The birthplace of the skyscraper and architecture on the planet, Chicago is city where dreams come true. Maybe i and support inherent in Midwesterners. from nicknames like "Second City", pushing us to strive to be number one. Maybe it's our tough-as-nails mentality honed over years of brutal winters. Whatever it is, rather than race to one-up each other, people here want to help each other succeed.

A wise friend once told me that Chicago is the quintessential American city: it's chock-full of a hard working ethos, that famed Midwestern niceness and the juxtaposition of old and new on nearly every street. With over 70 neighborhoods, it's home to one of the most diverse populations in the US. It's the ultimate melting pot, but beyond that it's a place where people – and their dreams – are welcomed, supported and celebrated.

matt kirouac
writer

When it came time to move away for college, the choice destination was obvious to New Hampshire native Matt Kirouac: Chicago. After earning a culinary degree from Robert Morris University, he became a food writer, has written for various publications, and has served as the associate editor for *Plate Magazine*. Away from his laptop, Matt enjoys bowling, walking his dogs around Ukrainian Village and being overly competitive when playing video games with his husband.

bradley kirouac
photographer

Born in Detroit and raised in Chicago, Bradley Kirouac fell in love with photography in Mrs Belf's AP art class, which prompted and inspired him to explore art in a new medium behind the lens. Even while serving in the US Marine Corps, he was rarely seen without a camera. Bradley enjoys long walks down the aisles of local produce markets and sunsets at the drive-in. He enjoys playing video games with his overly competitive husband, but since he's a better loser, is happy to come in second.

where to lay
your weary head

Rest up, relax and recharge

ACME HOTEL COMPANY

ACME HOTEL COMPANY

Hip downtown accommodation

15 East Ohio Street (between North State and North Wabash)
+1 312 894 0800 / acmehotelcompany.com

Double from $254

In terms of downtown hotels, there's a lot more than pomp and circumstance. For instance, the upscale hostel environment of ACME Hotel Company is as colorful and dynamic as a comic book come to life. Various vinyl collections decorate the lobby, The Berkshire Room (see pg 84) − one of the top cocktail lounges in town − is in the back, and the modish rooms and suites upstairs boast hardwood floors: a nice, swanky touch.

CHICAGO ATHLETIC ASSOCIATION HOTEL

Bygone institution brought back to life

12 South Michigan Avenue (between East Madison and East Monroe)
+1 312 940 3552 / chicagoathletichotel.com

Double from $160

Fusing the past with the present, this downtown hotel is a revamped property that originally took shape in the 1890s, but sat defunct on Michigan Avenue for decades. Now thoroughly polished and reopened, the Venetian Gothic-style, 13-story palace is once again the gem of the Loop, boasting unparalleled views of Millennium Park, immaculate rooms and some of the best hotel dining and drinking spaces in town. In a nod to its name and the fact that it once served as a club for Olympic athletes, the hotel has even transformed old basketball courts and swimming pools into grand event spaces.

GUESTHOUSE HOTEL

Homey, stylish digs

4872 North Clark Street (between West Lawrence and West Ainslie)
+1 773 564 9568 / theguesthousehotel.com

One bedroom suite from $348

A world apart from glamorous downtown, Guesthouse Hotel in Andersonville is more of an intimate bed & breakfast. Originally constructed as condos, the building was transformed into a chic inn with a club room, a spa and suites in all sizes, each one lending the feel of an upscale local apartment. Considering all the elegant touches like fireplaces, balconies and pristine kitchens, you may never want to leave.

CHICAGO ATHLETIC ASSOCIATION HOTEL

PUBLIC HOTEL

HOTEL LINCOLN

Artsy pad near the park

1816 North Clark Street (at North Wells and North Lincoln)
+1 312 254 4700 / jdvhotels.com/hotels/illinois/chicago-hotels/hotel-lincoln

Double from $195

Thirteen-story hotels infused with history must be a thing here, because Hotel Lincoln is another fine example of the form. Housed in a building that dates from the 1920s, this boutique property has been transformed and updated to fit a slick, modern aesthetic. Much of that can be attributed to the hotel's emphasis on art, which can be seen through a wide collection of pieces, mostly from local artists. The property is colorful inside and out, from the bustling ground floor and coffee shop to the bike rentals for guests, rooftop bar and the stylish rooms overlooking Lincoln Park and Lake Michigan.

LONGMAN & EAGLE

Sleep at the bar

2657 North Kedzie Avenue (at West Schubert)
+1 773 276 7110 / longmanandeagle.com

Double from $195

The offbeat inn atop Longman & Eagle is a modern ode to tavern abodes of yore, where boozed up patrons would rest their heads after a debaucherous night. The six upstairs rooms are a funky and cozy option, like fashionable urban dorm rooms that are in close proximity to the bustling downstairs restaurant and bar. However, the inn does caution visitors that whisky-fueled noise from downstairs can occasionally get raucous. But that adds to the fun.

PUBLIC HOTEL

Lounge in luxury

1301 North State Street (at West Goethe)
+1 312 787 3700 / publichotels.com

Double from $280

Do you fantasize about living like the most elite members of society? Well now you can, thanks to the Public Hotel. For a night or two, anyway. Nestled in the posh environs of mansion-packed Gold Coast, these updated digs still nod to the past and attract a high society crowd with its 285 luxurious guest rooms. The updated Pump Room menu was created by celebrity chef Jean-Georges Vongerichten, and the lobby-level library bar, featuring deep leather couches and craft cocktails, offers the most coveted seat in the house.

logan square

This northwest-side neighborhood has come a long way. Originally named for American soldier John A. Logan, it was a bustling neighborhood until the 1930s, when the population began to move away, leaving the area to fall into disrepair. Today, Logan Square is known less for dirt-cheap bodegas and more for its twee baristas and mustachioed mixologists, and has become the poster child for gentrification in Chicago. The sprawling hipster 'hood boasts some of the coolest shops in town, not to mention hot restaurants, buzzing bars and a vibrant nightlife scene. Its brusque roots may have been polished over, but Logan Square still maintains a sense of history, as evidenced by old-school jewelers, the omnipresence of Pabst Blue Ribbon and row upon row of timeworn boulevard mansions.

1 Bang Bang Pie & Biscuits   6 Lula Café
2 City Lit Books   7 Owen + Alchemy
3 Gaslight Coffee Roasters   8 Parson's Chicken & Fish
4 Logan Hardware   9 The Bird's Nest Salon
5 Lost Lake   10 Wolfbait & B-girls

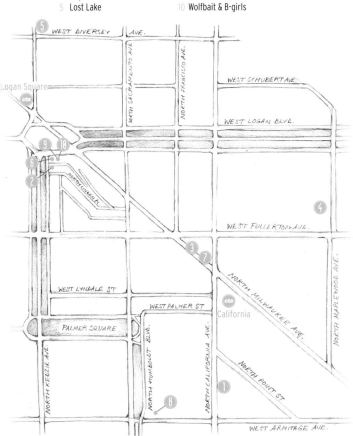

BANG BANG PIE & BISCUITS

A slice of Americana

2051 North California Avenue (between North Point and West Francis)
+1 773 276 8888 / bangbangpie.com / Closed Monday

Certain establishments exude good vibes. Bang Bang Pie & Biscuits is one of them. Where to begin? The coffee that costs a reasonable few bucks and doesn't require the irritatingly long wait for a chichi pour-over. The rickety furniture made from reclaimed wood. The colorful garden bedecked with picnic tables. The adorable pie carriers. And of course, the pie itself, available in seasonal flavors like blueberry, key lime and Superbowl (pretzel, chocolate and malted marshmallow). But the incomparable biscuits are even better than the pies. They are heavenly, fluffy and made all the more ethereal by the inclusion of sour cream in the dough. If you need a reason to travel to Logan Square, these biscuits are it

CITY LIT BOOKS

Book lovers, rejoice

2523 North Kedzie Boulevard (at North Linden) / **+1 773 235 2523**
citylitbooks.com / **Closed Monday**

It's a ballsy move to open a bookstore in this day and age, but owner
Teresa Kirschbraun did it unflinchingly in the summer of 2012. City Lit Books
is just the kind of place to remind you how much you miss indie bookshops.
When you walk in, the first thing that greets you is a table full of gorgeous
cookbooks, which always beckons me to browse. Then there are the
handwritten and oh-so-charming notes about recent favorite reads by
staffers, the Chicago lit section and an intimate area for readings with
visiting authors. It's all familiar, but somehow now feels like the best kind
of nostalgia.

GASLIGHT COFFEE ROASTERS

House-roasted brews with a side of taxidermy

2385 North Milwaukee Avenue (between West Fullerton and West Medill) / No phone / gaslightcoffeeroasters.com / Open daily

Walking up Milwaukee Avenue, I detect a hint of smoke in the air. At first I'm momentarily concerned – as I always am when I get a whiff of smoke – that something is actually on fire, and I flash back to the charred remains of my childhood home when it went up in flames some 20 years ago. Thankfully that isn't the case. The smell is the toasty aroma of freshly roasted beans wafting out of Gaslight Coffee Roasters, the best coffee shop in coffee shop-saturated Logan Square. The café's design is akin to a chic hunting lodge, and taxidermy is as prominent as laptops here, where java fiends flock for their artisanal caffeine fix before grappling over precious seat space. And the drinks? Delicious.

LOGAN HARDWARE

Record store and arcade museum

2532 West Fullerton Avenue (at North Maplewood) / **+1 773 235 5030**
logan-hardware.com / **Open daily**

Don't let the name of this shop deceive you: you won't find any home repair
fixtures at Logan Hardware anymore. Only the memory of the bygone
hardware store lives on in the business name, along with the vintage sign
on the exterior brick wall. Today, to the excitement of anyone who isn't a
handyman, this store is actually a record shop stocked to the gills with new
and vintage vinyl. Perhaps the coolest thing about it is the secret arcade
with retro pinball machines and other bygone accoutrements such as
cassette decks, vintage books and old-fashioned suitcases in the back room.

LOST LAKE

Taste the tropics

3154 West Diversey Avenue (between North Kedzie and North Troy)
+1 773 293 6048 / lostlaketiki.com / Open daily

Red-hot, tropical cocktails waned in popularity for decades, which seems odd to me – who in their right mind wouldn't want a drink that tastes like vacation? All hail mixologist Paul McGee, who captained the ship in terms of Chicago's tiki renaissance. His tribute to tiki bars of yore is a pint-sized paradise, illuminated with a glowing fish tank, vivid cocktail umbrellas, tropically clad servers and lavishly garnished libations in whimsical glassware. Fasten your mouth to a twirly straw and dive into the rum-, coconut- and passion fruit-based Tic-Tac-Taxi, then pair it with some chow fun noodles and handcrafted sarcastic fortune cookies from adjoining Chinese spot, Thank You.

LULA CAFÉ

Where food, cocktails and community converge

2537 North Kedzie Avenue (between West Logan and North Linden)
+1 773 489 9554 / lulacafe.com / Closed Tuesday

Long before this area became the foodie magnet it is today, Lula Café was the neighborhood's sole chef-driven restaurant, with extraordinary food and renowned prix fixe "farm dinners". Those days are long gone, but Lula has done more than keep up. It overhauled half of its space with a sleek expanded bar area, doubling its size to accommodate growing crowds, and the menu features an assortment of old standbys – including my favorite Chicago comfort food, salsa rossa, a spaghetti dish with bacon and chili – alongside seasonal specials, feverishly popular brunch creations and masterful cocktails. The neighborhood may have evolved enormously, but Lula remains the tentpole.

OWEN + ALCHEMY

Juice with style

2355 North Milwaukee Avenue (between West Fullerton and West Medill) / +1 773 227 3444 / owenandalchemy.com / Open daily

Imagine that Wednesday Addams grew up, attended fashion school, developed a penchant for cold-pressed fruits and veggies and decided to sling juices. The mental image you're conjuring is likely pretty similar to Owen + Alchemy, a darkly elegant and stylish juice bar on one of Logan Square's hottest blocks. Presided over by Anne Owen, Owen + Alchemy is billed as a modern day apothecary, decked out with a plant-lined wall, a library of glass bottled juices and nut milks, Hippocrates quotes and trinkets you'd expect to find in a Wiccan store. Chef Jared Van Camp contributes a thoughtful vegetarian menu, which complements the standout kale-based green juice, jet-black charcoal lemonade and a sweet blueberry-basil concoction.

PARSON'S CHICKEN & FISH

Laid-back food and Cali vibes

2952 West Armitage Avenue (between North Humboldt and North Richmond) / +1 773 384 3333 / parsonschickenandfish.com
Open daily

With its white-washed façade, beachy patio and boozy comforts, Parson's Chicken & Fish channels a welcome dose of vitamin D and brings vitamin N (Negroni slushies) to Chicago. The menu is a party in and of itself, with picnic-y crowd-pleasers like buckets of fried chicken, spicy pimento toast, creamy coleslaw, beer-battered fish sandwiches and ham-flecked hush puppies. All are best enjoyed alongside those aforementioned slushies and peppery micheladas while lounging on the expansive back patio. Wait times can be gruelling, but worthwhile when the end results are this joyous.

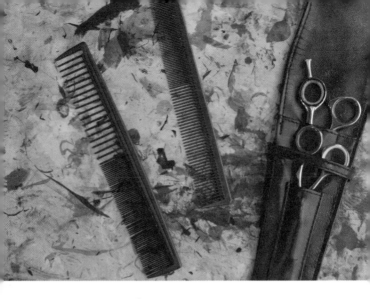

THE BIRD'S NEST SALON

Go blonde while staying green

3131 West Logan Boulevard (between North Milwaukee and North Kedzie) / +1 773 402 8126 / thebns.co / Closed Monday

So you want to change your hair, but don't want the products to be toxic. Head to this eco-friendly salon, where you can enjoy the view of Logan Square out of the soaring windows as well as deliciously witty banter with owner Gina Dominguez and her staff. It's a spot that pays as much attention to style as it does to its philosophies, which go above and beyond with environmentally conscious décor, products and recycling programs. So while you're fawning over your new 'do in the mirror, you can rest easy knowing it's not at all harmful to either you or the world around you.

WOLFBAIT & B-GIRLS

Indie wares with attitude

3131 West Logan Boulevard (between North Milwaukee and North Kedzie) / +1 312 698 8685 / wolfbaitchicago.com / Open daily

Wolfbait & B-girls sounds like a badass rock group full of riot grrrls, and the storefront feels like the backstage dressing room for one, too. All the eclectic goods sold here come from local designers who lend their talents to everything from soaps and syrups to shirts, signs and bracelets fashioned from pencils. It's the only place I shop for birthday presents, and my friends appreciate me dearly for my endless array of snarky coffee sleeves (because sipping coffee with a sleeve that reads "bitch" is just so much more enjoyable) and wine stoppers bedecked with mini terrariums. Owners/artists Shirley Kienitz and Jenny Stadler are unfailingly welcoming and sweet, a comical juxtaposition to throw pillows emblazoned with "I'm F—king Perf".

lincoln square

Stroll up Lincoln Avenue on Chicago's north side
and you'll find yourself dazzled by a heavily
European-accented enclave that's been carefully
preserved – more than any other neighborhood,
this is a sliver of old-world Chicago in the midst of
new-world modernity. Enduring relics are
everywhere, from the Davis Theater and iconic
French bistros to vintage toy stores, antique shops,
community fountains and other charming niceties
you'd sooner expect of a Norman Rockwell painting
than the middle of Chicago. While Lincoln Square
honors its past, the new guard brings forth striking
progression in the form of elaborate tasting menus,
some of the city's best Thai restaurants and most
forward-thinking markets.

1 Baker Miller
2 Chicago Brauhaus
3 Davis Theater
4 Elizabeth
5 Enjoy
6 Gene's Sausage Shop
  & Delicatessen
7 Merz Apothecary
8 Old Town School of Folk Music
9 Rainbow Thai Cuisine
10 Timeless Toys

BAKER MILLER

Confection heaven

4610 North Western Avenue (between West Wilson and West Eastwood)
+1 312 208 5639 / bakermillerchicago.com / Closed Monday

Before I got married, friends and colleagues chimed in on where I should get my wedding cake and who should make it. Though I appreciated their recommendations, to me, the answer was obviously Baker Miller. The husband-wife team behind this bakery and millhouse effortlessly toes the line between rustic and elegant. I first fell in love when they opened Bang Bang Pie & Biscuits (see pg 12), before decamping to broaden their baking breadth here. Not only did they create the double-tier Bundt wedding cake of my dreams, but on a daily basis they mill their own locally sourced grains to cook up the dreamiest oatmeal, the creamiest grits, the sweetest sourdough cinnamon rolls and the most delightful loaves. Swoon.

CHICAGO BRAUHAUS

German flair on the square

4732 North Lincoln Avenue (between West Leland and West Lawrence) / +1 773 784 4444 / chicagobrauhaus.com
Closed Tuesday

In step with many other businesses in the heart of Lincoln Square, Chicago Brauhaus feels more like a time capsule than a bar. The pivotal difference with this decades-old mainstay? There's a good risk of a hangover. But it's worth it for the flavorful gaiety found at this prominent German dining and drinking hall. Open in its current location since 1984, this woodsy lodge of a restaurant shows everyone a good time, with a tried-and-true formula of beer steins the size of my thigh, stellar wiener schnitzel, hot pretzels and folksy music courtesy of the Brauhaus Trio. Don't resist the urge to hit the dance floor.

DAVIS THEATER

The all-American movie-going experience

4614 North Lincoln Avenue (between West Wilson and West Eastwood) / +1 773 769 3999 / davistheater.com / Open daily

In a world riddled with 3-D movies, IMAX and buckets of popcorn that cost, well, a bucket, there's something wistful about a good old-fashioned movie theater. I crave the throwback Americana experience of squeaky cushioned seats, a velvet curtain covering the screen, tunnel-like hallways and an egregious amount of Sno Caps. The venerable red brick Davis Theater, whose iconic sign still stands as a beacon in Lincoln Square, satiates that craving and then some. The films shown at this four-screen cinema may be modern, but it's the perfect outlet to scratch that nostalgia itch. Because there's nothing better than laughing and crying in a theater that's nearly a century old. It's a cinematic ideal, especially when I'm tired of 3-D glasses-induced headaches.

ELIZABETH

Forest-to-table dining

4835 North Western Avenue (between West Lawrence and West Ainslie)
+1 773 681 0651 / elizabeth-restaurant.com / Closed Sunday and Monday

Iliana Regan infuses whimsy and excitement into her cuisine at Elizabeth, where eating gets interesting: during one of my visits, a course entailed crumbling food in your fist and "punching" yourself in the mouth in order to eat it. I first met Iliana at her underground restaurant One Sister, where elaborate, hours-long degustations were de rigueur. But the key was how Iliana always made her guests feel like kids at Willy Wonka's factory. One Sister eventually begot Elizabeth, where Iliana takes her masterful techniques to the next level in what she calls "new gatherer" cuisine. It's food she often forages herself in the Midwest, resulting in dishes that run the gamut from edible insects to mushrooms to bear. It's one knockout of an experience.

ENJOY

Irreverant gifts and sundries

4723 North Lincoln Avenue (between West Leland and West Lawrence) / +1 773 334 8626 / urbangeneralstore.com / Open daily

Growing up, my idea of a general store was a place at the end of the street where I could pick up bottles of Yoo-hoo. The throwback concept of a local corner store gets turned on its head at Enjoy, an "urban general store" in Lincoln Square's most charming corridor. I can forgive their lack of Yoo-hoo considering how much the shop makes me giggle. The array of quirky artisan wares never ceases to disappoint. My hands-down favorite is an avenging unicorn designed to impale different figurines as a means of relieving stress, but I also love the squirrel feeders, bacon bandages and, for the dark-humored among us, shower curtains featuring bloody handprints that look like something out of *Psycho*.

GENE'S SAUSAGE SHOP & DELICATESSEN

Much more than encased meat

4750 North Lincoln Avenue (between West Lawrence and West Leland) / +1 773 728 7243 / genessausage.com / Open daily

Gene's Sausage Shop & Delicatessen is home to more than 30 sausage varieties – all made from house-butchered meats that are smoked on the premises – but they do have more than just bangers. The place makes grocery shopping fun with a wide inventory that boasts a dizzying variety of prepared foods, imported goods, pastries, breads and even liquor. It's also a reliable spot to pick up German limburger and elderberry syrup in a pinch. This family-run institution originally took shape in a much smaller form in the '70s, before christening a new era with this sprawling storefront in 2009. When the weather's nice, enjoy a pint or a glass of wine in their rooftop beer garden.

MERZ APOTHECARY

Retro druggist, modern wellness

4716 North Lincoln Avenue (between West Leland and West Lawrence)
+1 773 989 0900 / merzapothecary.com / Closed Sunday

Conceptualized in the 1800s by pharmacist Peter Merz, this drugstore
evolved over the years at different locations before settling on its Lincoln
Square home in 1982. Walking into the preserved-in-time store is the
closest to that kid-in-the-candy-shop feeling you can find in Chicago,
assuming your idea of "candy" is pharmaceuticals. Merz sells thousands of
products – from face wash and lotions to perfume, candles and digestives
– with a solid section devoted to naturopathic medicines. You've never
seen so many toothpastes, lip balms or natural deodorants in your life,
and chances are, you haven't heard of these mostly European versions. In
business for nearly 150 years, Merz is doing something right.

OLD TOWN SCHOOL OF FOLK MUSIC

Intimate concerts for all ages

4544 North Lincoln Avenue (between West Sunnyside and West Wilson) / +1 773 728 6000 / oldtownschool.org / Open daily

"I think I'm going to start taking djembe lessons," my friend said one recent evening. "Where?" I asked, knowing the answer could only be the Old Town School of Folk Music. The West African drumming technique, along with global and regional American musical practices, are celebrated and showcased in multiple ways at this esteemed music haven. While classes are available for pretty much anything that makes rhythmic noise, the best way to interact with the school (at least for the layperson) is through a concert. Unlike frenzied music halls, the shows here are much more intimate and subdued, keeping the spotlight squarely on the art of making music. It also hosts music festivals and stocks a store filled with guitars, ukuleles, mandolins, keyboards and more.

RAINBOW THAI CUISINE

A whole lot of spice and everything nice

4825 North Western Avenue (between West Lawrence and West Ainslie) / +1 773 754 7660 / rainbowthaichicago.com / Closed Monday

Thai food is a form of masochism for me. The more it sears my taste buds, the better. It's not about ruthless spice for the sake of tongue torture at Rainbow Thai Cuisine, though – it's more refined than that. Heat is applied in moderation alongside pungent components like sour, sweet and funky. The flavor stars align at this blink-and-you'll-miss-it Thai spot, where you'll find the usual noodle and rice dishes you'd expect. Ask for the special menu to plunge down the rabbit hole into a world of bold tastes with dishes like housemade sai krog i-san (fermented sausage), nam khao tod (crispy rice salad with soured pork) and phla kung (prawn salad). In this instance, the phrase "taste the rainbow" is a lot more potent than Skittles.

TIMELESS TOYS

Playful nostalgia

4749 North Lincoln Avenue (between West Lawrence and West Leland) / +1 773 334 4445 / timelesstoyschicago.com / Open daily

I first heard about Timeless Toys from my friend Angelina Jolie. Okay, so technically I read about her visiting the vintage toy store in a local paper, but let it be known that Angelina has great taste because this mom-and-pop is as whimsical and wonderful as they come. Owners Harry and Martha Burrows, who moonlight as puppeteers, may as well be the real life Santa and Mrs Claus, because their shop recalls quaint imagery of the North Pole. Every corner glistens with color and hums with life. Embrace your inner child and get lost in a *Where's Waldo* book, play with figurines ranging from *Star Wars* characters to classic knights and archers, and cuddly stuffed animals. It's Angelina-approved, after all.

magnificent museums
More than just art

CHICAGO'S CHILDREN MUSEUM

Chicago's museum scene is one of the best in the country. There's everything from the encyclopedic Art Institute of Chicago to the Museum Campus, where a natural history museum, aquarium and planetarium are steps away from each other, as well as niche gems such as the Swedish American Museum (see pg 43), Museum of Broadcast Communications (see pg 82) and the National Museum of Mexican Art (see pg 112). But there are a few lesser-known museums here that are well worth your time.

My absolute favorite is the incredible **Museum of Science and Industry**. Housed in the former Palace of Fine Arts, the sole remaining building from the 1893 World's Columbian Exposition, this is the largest science museum in the western hemisphere, packed with mesmeric exhibits and experiences like a defunct war submarine, an underground coal mine and a modern, illuminated mirror maze that looks like something out of a Daft Punk video.

The **Chicago Children's Museum** is a great place to take the whole brood. Not only is it dazzling and entertaining for all ages, but it handily cloaks education in fun, encouraging hands-on interaction, whether it's digging up fossils at the dinosaur exhibit or by learning fire safety aboard the fire truck.

CHICAGO CHILDREN'S MUSEUM
700 East Grand Avenue (east of Lake Shore Drive
on Navy Pier), +1 312 527 1000
chicagochildrensmuseum.org, open daily

**DUSABLE MUSEUM OF AFRICAN
AMERICAN HISTORY**
740 East 56th Place (between South Cottage Grove
and Payne), +1 773 947 0600, dusablemuseum.org
closed Monday

MUSEUM OF CONTEMPORARY ART
220 East Chicago Avenue (between Mies van der
Rohe and North Fairbanks), +1 312 280 2660
mcachicago.org, closed Monday

MUSEUM OF SCIENCE AND INDUSTRY
5700 South Lake Shore Drive (between East 57th
and South Cornell), +1 773 684 1414
msichicago.org, open daily

When in town, you really shouldn't miss the **DuSable Museum of African
American History**, which serves as a thorough homage to African American
culture. Check out Red, White, Blue & Black, an exhibit examining the history of
African Americans in the armed forces, and the Africa Speaks area, lined with
myriad artifacts from Africa and its people.

The boundary-pushing **Museum of Contemporary Art** dares to probe with
emotional exhibits covering events like September 11, 2001, and figures such
as Frida Kahlo and David Bowie. The multi-floor space also contains a theater
for musical performances and a fantastic gift shop, featuring items like a scarf
made from refurbished wood pieces, which has single-handedly garnered more
compliments for me than anything else I've ever worn.

andersonville

Nestled amidst the upper reaches of the city, a stone's throw from the shores of Lake Michigan, you'll find Andersonville, a charming enclave hustling and bustling with chic stores, brick abodes, quaint cafés and timeworn restaurants. The area honors its historical Scandinavian roots – think buildings and signage emblazoned with the Swedish flag, along with restaurants serving Nordic fare and a culture museum – while looking to the future with novel businesses that give the cozy neighborhood sensation fresh new meaning.

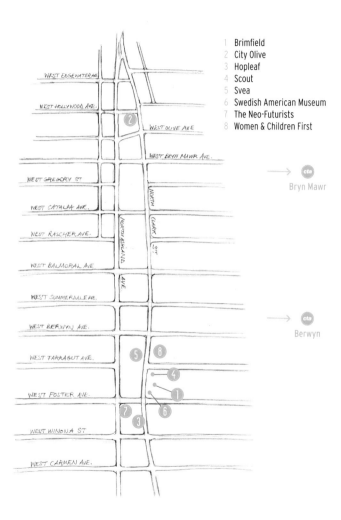

1 Brimfield
2 City Olive
3 Hopleaf
4 Scout
5 Svea
6 Swedish American Museum
7 The Neo-Futurists
8 Women & Children First

cta
Bryn Mawr

cta
Berwyn

BRIMFIELD

Homewares for lovers of vintage

5219 North Clark Street (between West Foster and West Farragut)
+1 773 271 3501 / brimfieldus.com / **Open daily**

I suspect that Julie Fernstrom pillaged my childhood attic to stock Brimfield, where everything from seashell collections to Santa-shaped mugs and wooden skis are on deck. Though it's a shop, Brimfield feels like home to me, awash as it is in warm plaid scarves and blankets, stuffed animals, reupholstered furniture, American flag paraphernalia and some of the most stylish taxidermy, including pheasants with bow ties and mounted deer heads draped with scarves. Just make sure to give yourself enough time to browse once you get your bearings; the storefront spills into an adjoining garage and basement.

CITY OLIVE

Andersonville's Mediterranean oasis

5644 North Clark Street (between West Olive and West Hollywood)
+1 773 942 6424 / **cityolive.com** / **Closed Monday**

If you regard olive oils with the same ravenous vigor as Belle's adoration
for books in *Beauty and the Beast*, prepare to revel in City Olive, the
store that gives olive oil the spotlight it deserves. Radiating the feel of a
Mediterranean general store, this place is all about the nourishing lipids,
featuring shelf after shelf of gourmet olive oils from the likes of Greece,
Portugal, New Zealand, Chile, the US and more. But since man can't live
on olive oil alone (I've tried), the shop also stocks a hodgepodge of other
provisions – think tapenades, mustards, vinaigrettes and chocolates –
perfect to spruce up a picnic or a dinner party.

HOPLEAF

European beer bastion

5148 North Clark Street (between West Winona and West Foster)
+1 773 334 9851 / hopleafbar.com / Open daily

I often wonder if I can hide away in one of Hopleaf's dimly lit nooks and never leave. From the life-affirming, beer-steamed mussels to the extensive array of brews, and the dark, lodge-like feel of the meandering space, Hopleaf is the epitome of comfort. It helps that the timeworn pub also does a helluva job reminding me of a rustic wizard bar out of Harry Potter's Hogsmeade village. But I digress. This is a longtime Andersonville staple, esteemed by customers like myself who fawn over those aforementioned mussels with cultish obsession. The place just gets better with age, implementing new additions like lunch service and expanded space to help mitigate wait times.

SCOUT

Fun antiques for your home

5221 North Clark Street (at West Farragut) / +1 773 275 5700
scoutchicago.com / Closed Monday

I'd never really felt that my apartment was lacking in marlin, but thanks to unique home store Scout, I now know that's the case. When I come here, I always uncover decorative inspirations I never before knew I needed. Like the previously mentioned giant marlin wall fixture. Or a typewriter that I'm just desperate to tinker with. Or a portrait of Thoreau done entirely in tiny wood panels. You see, from wall décor and lighting to desk toppers, pillows and quirky picnic baskets, Scout does it all. Every item at this minimalist, modern shop is meticulously sourced by owner Larry Vodak with the precision of a paleontologist unearthing fossils. If you fall in love with something (spoiler alert: you will), act fast, because these goods don't stay long.

SVEA

Nostalgic Swedish diner

5236 North Clark Street (between West Farragut and West Berwyn)
+1 773 275 7738 / facebook.com/pages/Svea-Restaurant / Open daily

While some of Andersonville's Scandinavian roots have waned over the years (R.I.P. Swedish flag water tower), one legend stays strong. Svea remains the neighborhood's quintessential breakfast and lunch haunt, boasting Nordic home cooking like fruit soup, pickled herring, molasses-y limpa bread and meatballs aplenty. The space recalls a diner of yesteryear, but strictly in the sense that your idea of an old-school diner is decorated with Swedish flags and Viking paraphernalia. The breakfast counter, which is surely older than I am, is lined with swiveling bright blue stools. It's a comfy place to perch and nosh on falukorv, a plump bologna-like sausage from Sweden. And I could live off the rice pudding with lingonberries... that is, until my dentist performs an intervention.

SWEDISH AMERICAN MUSEUM

Journey through Chicago's Scandinavian history

5211 North Clark Street (between West Foster and West Farragut)
+1 773 728 8111 / swedishamericanmuseum.org / Open daily

With the attention span of a gnat, it takes a particular type of museum to grip me for more than a few minutes. Andersonville's emblematic Swedish American Museum, an homage to the neighborhood's beginnings, is such a place. Not only does it thoroughly depict the plight of the Scandinavian immigrant, but it's so deeply homey, it feels as if my grandma curated it herself. The multi-level museum features an array of exhibits for guests of all ages, from Nordic weaponry to the Brunk's Children's Museum of Immigration. Even the King of Sweden left impressed.

THE NEO-FUTURISTS

Introspective theater

5153 North Ashland Avenue (between West Foster and West Winona)
+1 773 878 4557 / neofuturists.org / Open Friday to Sunday

The Neo-Futurists theater company was conceived in 1988, and started out as Chicago's first late-night show, then upped the ante with the ambitious mission to perform 30 micro plays in 60 minutes. It sounds like a rapid-fire sketch show on par with *Saturday Night Live*, but there's a lot more complexity behind a performance here. To watch a show at this groundbreaking theater is to buckle up for a front-seat ride on a non-stop tour de force of comedic, emotional social commentary. Brevity and audience interaction are still the bread and butter of The Neo-Futurists, whose performances are more like theatrical therapy than typical live theater. Bonus: the theater manager orders pizza for sold-out audiences, which is always therapeutic.

WOMEN & CHILDREN FIRST

Indie bookstore with a side of feminism

5233 North Clark Street (at West Farragut) / **+1 773 769 9299**
womenandchildrenfirst.com / **Open daily**

It sounds a lot like the "feminist bookstore" skit from *Portlandia* for a reason: Women & Children First is the very store the show was spoofing. This heartwarming neighborhood keystone chock-full of unabashed feminist literature, kid lit and LGBTQ offerings is the real deal: an Andersonville icon heralded by minorities and celebrated by feminists. The space reminds me of my elementary school library, albeit with more spunk, complete with a playful children's area and scheduled reading events. Although ownership changed hands over the years, the enduring shop has maintained its core philosophy and remains a neighborhood bastion; the type of place where all feel welcome and cherished.

eat like a local

Because Chicago-style is a way of life

PEQUOD'S PIZZA

When people think of food in Chicago, the two dishes that come to mind first are deep-dish pizza and hot dogs. While not every joint is worth your stomach space, there are some gems scattered throughout the city that showcase just how seriously we take our food.

Pequod's Pizza in Lincoln Park is a dim tavern with a deep-dish secret weapon: a caramelized crust that achieves blissful new levels of doughy satisfaction. When piled with tangy tomato sauce and fresh veggies, it becomes one of the finest examples of pizza in town.

It may look modest, but **The Art of Pizza** truly does make an art form of the deep-dish. Here, the crust is taller, sturdier and firmer (this makes for the yummiest leftovers!), laying a solid foundation for a decadent striation of tomatoes, gooey cheese and pepperoni.

In Hyde Park, **Medici on 57th** has had more than 50 years to hone their technique. Both the pan and thin crust pizzas are soulful and sinful in the same bite. Take the signature Garbage Pizza, for instance, laden with sausage, ground beef, pepperoni, Canadian bacon, peppers, onion, mushrooms, and immersed in a layer of mozzarella and marinara. See what I mean?

Chicago-style hot dogs, traditionally heaped with yellow mustard, white onions, a pickle spear, neon-green relish, celery salt, sport peppers and a tomato in a poppy-seed bun, are best enjoyed in a classic throwback environment. Get your fix at **Red Hot Ranch**, a dive-y hot dog stand in Bucktown with a simplified menu of plump hot dogs, crispy fries and spicy Polish sausages.

FATSO'S LAST STAND
2258 West Chicago Avenue (between North Oakley and
North Leavitt), +1 773 245 3287, fatsoslaststand.com
open daily

MEDICI ON 57TH
1327 East 57th Street (between South Kenwood and
South Kimbark), +1 773 667 7394, medici57.com
open daily

PEQUOD'S PIZZA
2207 North Clybourn Avenue (between West Webster
and North Greenview), +1 773 327 1512
pequodspizza.com, open daily

RED HOT RANCH
2072 North Western Avenue (between West Dickens
and West Charleston), +1 773 772 6020, no website
open daily

SUPERDAWG DRIVE-IN
6363 North Milwaukee Avenue (at West Devon)
+1 773 763 0660, superdawg.com, open daily

THE ART OF PIZZA
3033 North Ashland Avenue (between West Nelson
and West Barry), +1 773 327 5600, artofpizzainc.com
open daily

The name may elicit chuckles, but **Fatso's Last Stand** in Ukrainian Village is no laughing matter. Not in terms of the seriousness with which they approach their charred hot dogs – with buns split down the center and grilled to garner a toasty, succulent texture – hamburgers and crunchy fried shrimp.

It doesn't get any more classic than the humongous glowing hot dog mascots positioned above **Superdawg Drive-In** on Chicago's far northwest side. Try the namesake Superdawg, outfitted with chopped Spanish onions and piccalilli, and served with the most addictive crinkle-cut French fries in existence.

lincoln park

Rife with mansions, tree-lined streets, college campuses and one of the most serene city parks in the country, Lincoln Park is a stunner of a neighborhood situated a stone's throw from the nexus of Chicago's downtown urban jungle. Anchored by the namesake park, a miles-long lakeside haven of sports fields, beaches, farmers' markets, museums and a zoo, Lincoln Park is a family-friendly escape that is completely unlike the rest of the city. Where else can you marvel at lions, play beach volleyball, peruse vintage furniture and sip a rooftop cocktail all in the same afternoon?

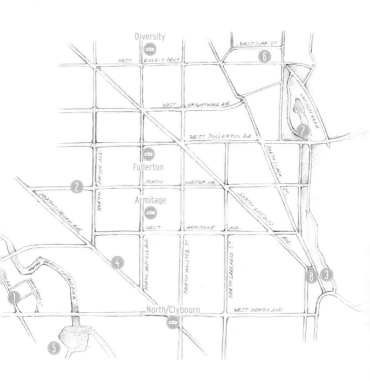

1 Ada Street	5 Kayak Chicago
2 Floriole Café & Bakery	6 mfk.
3 Green City Market	7 Peggy Notebaert Nature Museum
4 Jayson Home	8 The J. Parker

ADA STREET

Offbeat contemporary eats

1664 North Ada Street (between West Concord and West Wabansia) / **+1 773 697 7069** / adastreetchicago.com
Closed Monday

Walking into Ada Street, one of the most unexpected dining surprises in one of the most unassuming warehouse districts, it becomes immediately evident that this isn't your average dinner experience. The dark entry feels a bit like a haunted house: I half expected a ghost to leap out at me from some dark corner. Past the meandering hallway lined with vintage records you'll find a hip restaurant filled with standout dishes and snacks, such as fried black-eyed peas, polenta fries and salted chocolate toast for dessert. When it's warm out, the AstroTurf-lined patio is the place to be, especially if you're one for ping pong and picnic tables.

FLORIOLE CAFÉ & BAKERY

Delicious pastries and homey ambiance

1220 West Webster Avenue (between North Magnolia and North Racine) / +1 773 883 1313 / floriole.com / Closed Tuesday

If ever I stumbled upon a genie's lamp and could wish to live anywhere in Chicago, it unquestionably would be Floriole Café & Bakery. During the seemingly endless winters, the sun-flooded, two-story space offers a perfect hideaway to recharge with a book, a cappuccino and a BAD (bacon, arugula, date) sandwich on fluffy cornmeal bread. What started out as a farmers' market vendor has evolved into one of the city's quintessential cafés, a French-inspired masterpiece with a rooftop garden, killer almond croissants and some of the most scrumptious brownies I've ever had the pleasure of shoveling into my mouth at a greedy rate. In warmer weather, the expansive front doors open onto the sidewalk, which is where you'll find me merrily making use of their Wi-Fi for hours on end.

GREEN CITY MARKET

Organic and natural groceries

1800 North Clark Street (inside Lincoln Park) / +1 773 880 1266
greencitymarket.org / Open Wednesday and Saturday (summer)
2430 North Cannon Drive (north of West Fullerton Parkway)
Open Saturday (winter)

Waking up early on a Saturday morning and hauling to Green City Market with a stash of tote bags used to be my favorite summer activity. But now that the market runs every Saturday throughout the winter (November to April) inside the Peggy Notebaert Nature Museum (see pg 56), a weekly visit to Chicago's preeminent farmers' market is one of my favorite activities year-round. There's a reason that chefs from the city's finest restaurants stock up on seasonal fare here, and it's not the stellar smoothies, scrumptious crêpes or Neapolitan pizzas cooked to order. None of those hurt, but the reason the kitchen honchos come is because the produce is possibly the best in town.

JAYSON HOME

Modern and vintage housewares galore

1885 North Clybourn Avenue (between North Kenmore and North Sheffield) / +1 773 248 8180 / jaysonhome.com / Open daily

I'm going to be honest: if I thought I could get away with it, I would make a beeline to Jayson Home and pillage their inventory. With a wide range of both contemporary and antique home décor, this Lincoln Park shop feels like stepping inside an issue of *Dwell* magazine. Nestled along the bustling Clybourn Corridor, this store stands out as a lofty oasis of cool, uncommon finds that run the gamut from garden accents and regal benches to antique statues, palatial rugs and stumps of petrified wood that would look mighty nice bookending the Gustav love seat of my dreams.

KAYAK CHICAGO

Magnificent views from the river

1220 West LeMoyne Avenue (at North Magnolia) / +1 312 852 9258
kayakchicago.com / Open daily

Considering the undeniable beauty of Lake Michigan and the mucky water
in the Chicago River, it seems an obvious choice to spend time coasting
at the lake (see pg 58) when it comes to aquatic activities here. But one
trip rowing down the river, gawking up at towering buildings, will change
your mind. As stunning a view as the Chicago Architecture Boat Tour offers
(a classic touristy experience that's well worth the time, even for locals),
making your own way through the city by kayak is even more exhilarating.
Not to mention a good workout as you ride past the motor boats making
mini waves by your side. Just don't spend too much time looking at the
questionable water soaking your lap.

MFK.

Seafood with a Spanish accent

432 West Diversey Parkway (between North Pine Grove and North Sheridan) / +1 773 857 2540 / mfkrestaurant.com / Open daily

Lincoln Park may be far from any ocean, but you'd never know it considering the surfeit of city seagulls and the pristine freshness of nautical creations at this sunny gem of a restaurant. Named after legendary food writer M.F.K. Fisher, mfk. made a splash when it opened in 2014 as a restaurant boldly going where few Chicago restaurants have gone before. It's a seafood haunt that dares diners to gnaw on crunchy prawn heads with Salbitxada, go classic with tortilla Española with salt cod brandade, snack on anchovies and tear into whole portions of loup de mer. The shareable plates and beachy motif, including seashore art pieces and cute windows reminiscent of a beachside cottage, are as inviting as it gets.

PEGGY NOTEBAERT
NATURE MUSEUM

Earthy fun

2430 North Cannon Drive (north of West Fullerton Parkway)
+1 773 755 5100   naturemuseum.org   Open daily

As a kid, one of my most magical experiences was the larger-than-life
Honey, I Shrunk the Kids exhibit at Disney's Hollywood Studios, an immersive
playground jungle filled with plants, fake animals and giant blades of grass
doubling as slides. To my dismay, I recently learned that I am now too old to
visit – Disney's punishment for my lack of offspring. But I get the last laugh,
because the Peggy Notebaert Nature Museum achieves the same level of
interactive, awe-inducing whimsy and education disguised as fun. Stemming
from the Chicago Academy of Sciences, the museum is a charming Eden of
exploratory jungle-scapes, butterfly exhibits, outdoor trails, and more.
The best part? No age restrictions.

THE J. PARKER

Rooftop cocktails with a parkside view

**13th Floor Hotel Lincoln, 1816 North Clark Street
(at North Lincoln)** / **+1 312 254 4747** / jparkerchicago.com
Open daily

Chicago loves its rooftop bars, and there are many scattered throughout the cityscape. One that stands out is The J. Parker, a (mostly) outdoor bar perched atop the 13th floor of Lincoln Park's boutique Hotel Lincoln (see pg 8). As someone typically petrified of heights, 13 stories up is oddly comfortable for me. At least, it's comfortable enough for me to plant myself near the glass railings without succumbing to crippling acrophobia. Perhaps it has something to do with the dazzling vista of Lincoln Park, Lake Michigan and the downtown skyline. Or perhaps my senses are simply stupefied by seasonal cocktails like the Lush Life made with rum, coconut liqueur, cumin, lime and pineapple. Either way, I'm sitting pretty up here.

lakefront activities

Fun in the sun

12TH STREET BEACH
1200 South Linn White Drive (south of Museum Campus on Northerly Island), +1 773 363 2225 chicagoparkdistrict.com/parks/12th-street-beach open daily

CASTAWAYS
1603 North Lake Shore Drive (between North Avenue and Lake Michigan), +1 773 281 1200 castawayschicago.com, open daily

LAKEFRONT TRAIL
Along Lake Michigan, open daily

MAGIC HEDGE
4400 North Lake Shore Drive (between West Montrose and Lake Michigan), +1 312 742 5121 chicagoparkdistrict.com/parks/montrose-beach open daily

SOUTH SHORE CULTURAL TRAIL
7059 South South Shore Drive (between East 70th and East 71st), +1 773 256 0149, chicagoparkdistrict. com/parks/South-Shore-Cultural-Center open daily

12TH STREET BEACH

Few cities are as aquatically obsessed as Chicago. Maybe it's our lack of a sea view that makes us truly appreciate Lake Michigan, interacting with it in any way that we can, as often as we can.

You'd never really know we are bereft of an ocean, considering the endless lineup of sandy, lakeside beaches, complete with unruly seagulls and a saltwater breeze. Dip your toes in the waves at **12th Street Beach**: this serene hideaway is ideal for sunning and swimming and sandcastle-building.

One of the largest and most popular beaches in town also boasts one of the most calming nature-in-the-city adventures. Adorably known as **Magic Hedge**, the Montrose Beach Bird Sanctuary is a sprawling forest of nature trails. Expect to see birds of all sizes and colors, plus flowers aplenty, tall grass and the occasional finicky rabbit.

If you're going to dare to attempt North Avenue Beach, easily the most overrun and definitely the most MTV Spring Break, you'll need a cocktail. Head to the gigantic beached ship, transformed into a bi-level bar and restaurant called **Castaways**. The tropically inclined drinks are refreshing and vacation-y, especially the luscious Mai Tais, and the view of the skyline is impeccable.

From Edgewater on the north side, **Lakefront Trail** is an 18-mile pathway that descends to the southern stretches of the city. Along the way, whether you're biking, walking or rollerblading, you'll experience some of the best views the lakefront has to offer: Navy Pier, Grant Park, Museum Campus and many more sights line your route.

On the southern edge of Chicago's lakefront, you'll find the **South Shore Cultural Center**, a century-old designated historic landmark that spans nearly 70 acres. One of the standout features is the park's nine-hole golf course, a fun and scenic place to tee off if such sports don't infuriate you. There's also lots of green space for strolls and picnics, if that's more your speed.

wicker park

Once regarded as shady territory on Chicago's near
northwest side, Wicker Park has steadily and rapidly
evolved from grunge to hip. The gentrification has been
swift in this area – often referred to as the Brooklyn
of Chicago – as derelict spaces transformed into
restaurants, independent boutiques, jam-packed coffee
houses, dance studios and world-class bars.
The playground of the city's young, hip and trendy,
Wicker Park has come full-circle with a little bit of
everything for everyone. It maintains a gritty sense
of its artsy roots, as depicted via street art and ample
independent galleries, while also appealing to a wider
audience of new residents moving into condos, town
homes, lofts and walk-up apartments.

1 Antique Taco
2 Eskell
3 Iridium Clothing Co.
4 MANA Food Bar

5 Penelope's
6 Pub Royale
7 Transit Tees
8 Violet Hour

61

ANTIQUE TACO

Mexican eats and vintage treats

**1360 North Milwaukee Avenue (between North Wood and
North Paulina) / +1 773 687 8697 / antiquetaco.com / Closed Monday**

You don't have to be a vegetarian to lust over the market mushroom
taco with pickled escabeche, savory kale and creamy cilantro sauce at
Antique Taco. Does this mean I'd swear off the meat or fish options when
visiting here? Not a chance. With so many Mexican restaurants in this area,
it takes a little bit of something extra beyond delicious food to grab the
public's attention. This place does precisely that with its cozy shop-meets-
taqueria approach. Grab a rosemary-infused margarita and do a bit of
shopping while waiting for your meal to come – how fun is that?

ESKELL

Eclectic womenswear

1509 North Milwaukee Avenue (at North Honore)
+1 773 486 0830 / eskell.com / Open daily

Between the window displays made from Barbie dolls and oversized dream catchers, and the decorative touches like vintage camisoles hanging from doorknobs above the perfume display, a few things are clear about the Eskell ladies: they love the '80s (see heart-shaped sunglasses and leopard print dresses), they're a bit bohemian (find flasks and funky jewelry) and very romantic. All of these observations are reasons to shop here and celebrate the fun in fashion. But it's the eponymous line, Eskell, that's particularly notable. Silk shirts and dresses made from custom-printed, often Art Deco-inspired textiles convince shoppers to take on extra dry cleaning bills without wincing. And now that they've branched out into jewelry with a similar vibe, it's nearly impossible not to indulge.

IRIDIUM CLOTHING CO.

Trend-forward clothing and accessories

1330 North Milwaukee Avenue (between North Wood and North Paulina) / +1 312 775 2456 / iridiumclothingco.com / Open daily

Not to brag, but every time I put on an item from Iridium Clothing Co., I feel like I belong on the streets of LA being stalked by a paparazzo. The attire peddled at Iridium, a popular online brand-cum-store, is the stuff of a Hollywood starlet's Coachella fantasies. It's the rare shop where each and every item is uniquely designed and special, from artfully baggy shirts to flower-bedecked pants, John Lennon-esque sunglasses, patterned leggings and billowy ponchos. Most of the stuff here is for men, though some items are designed for women, and much of the inventory is what I'd consider gender-neutral.

MANA FOOD BAR

Seasonal vegetarian cuisine

1742 West Division Street (between North Hermitage and North Wood)
+1 773 342 1742 / manafoodbar.com / Open daily

Fiddlehead ferns are not exactly synonymous with the Chicago dining experience. This is, after all, a town where bright green pickle relish is considered a vegetable, and this furry, curly plant is nowhere to be found growing within city limits. But when you live near a place like MANA Food Bar, a craving for ferns and other vegetarian delights is a given. I'd unflinchingly bring any meat-eating friend to this place and challenge them not to leave fully sated. The sesame noodles, mushroom and brown rice sliders and creamy polenta dotted with sautéed mushrooms are addictive and lead me to believe that if every vegetarian restaurant operated with the panache of MANA, the world would be entirely happy going meat-free.

PENELOPE'S

Playful clothes for grown-ups

1913 West Division Street (between North Wolcott and North Winchester) / **+1 773 395 2351** / **shoppenelopes.com** / **Open daily**

Living in the Wicker Park vicinity, it's easy to feel like you've grown up with Penelope's husband-and-wife owners Joe and Gena Lauer. Ten years ago, the then fresh-out-of-college couple were dating and the shop catered to sprite young pixies. They pioneered the arrival of certain fashion lines in town, such as APC, Built by Wendy and those Freitag bags you see on shoulders everywhere. Now married with kids, the Lauers still enliven their shop with a youthful energy — you can always find a jumper, mini skirt or hot pants when you need 'em — but they've also introduced more sophisticated pieces like ankle boots and Filson bags for those days when you need to look like a real adult.

PUB ROYALE

Indian cuisine gets a boozy boost

2049 West Division Street (between North Hoyne and North Damen)
+1 773 661 6874 / pubroyale.com / Open daily

My love affair with Pub Royale started with the alcoholic mango lassi. I knew we'd be a perfect match when I heard of its rum-infused take on the classic Indian beverage: made with mango purée, yogurt, a dash of heady paprika and, of course, rum, it proved to be my quintessential summer cocktail, and was the tip of the iceberg in terms of savory discoveries at this Anglo-Indian bar. Housed in a boisterous and airy space that looks like a South Asian beach cabana, Pub Royale offers traditional Indian dining. The drinks, as mentioned, are epic, but so is the food. Salt cod samosas, butter paneer and rabbit pie pair wonderfully with the alluring potions on offer.

TRANSIT TEES

For those who love Chicago

1371 North Milwaukee Avenue (between North Wood and North Paulina) / +1 773 227 1810 / transittees.com / Open daily

On any given day, I avoid anything operated by the Chicago Transit Authority because of the crowds. I'll walk, bike and cab my way everywhere in order to steer clear of the congested train system. That said, if you avoid rush hour, some routes are scenic and can be fairly leisurely. Even so, considering how rarely I frequent public transportation, it's surprising then that I'm so smitten with Transit Tees, a Chicago-centric shop that puts a quirky spin on all things CTA with branded apparel, coasters, wall fixtures, bags and other urban accoutrements that give me a new perspective on my love/hate relationship with the city's transit system.

VIOLET HOUR

Chic cocktails

1520 North Damen Avenue (between West Le Moyne and West Pierce)
+1 773 252 1500 / theviolethour.com / Open daily

Violet Hour is less an upscale bar and more a whimsical hideaway of Wonderland proportions. While I have little tolerance for the tedious wait most nights of the week, the queue outside the unmarked bar is for good reason. The doorman only allows in as many guests as there are seats, which means you'll never find yourself hovering awkwardly with your date. Plus, the high-backed chairs, reminiscent of mad tea party fixtures, allow for intimate conversations. Good thing too, because the bartenders take their time with drinks, though the wait is worth it: between the tasty homemade bitters and fresh juice used in these cocktails, you'll want to savor your drink as long as you can.

CHICAGO AFTER DARK:
late night live

Laugh, groove, drink and dance

From Second City (you're welcome, *Saturday Night Live*) to The Green Mill, Chicago's late-night live comedy and music scenes are well documented. Such twilight entertainments are integral to a thorough Chicagoan experience, celebrated and showcased throughout city limits.

For the better part of a century, **The Green Mill** has been crooning and boozing in Uptown. Once frequented by Al Capone and his mobster mates, the jazz lounge still has smooth tunes, potent cocktails and a richly vintage vibe.

Jazz gets more upbeat at **Andy's Jazz Club** in River North. The downtown locale begets a club with more liveliness and clamor, interspersed with bites of burgers and jambalaya. The music is joyous, more in tune with gregarious New Orleans-style blues than the cerebral, hard-to-follow jazz you may be thinking of.

Things get grungier at the storied **Empty Bottle** in Ukrainian Village. This longstanding bar is a hot spot for intimate sets by roving indie bands. It's a neighborhood keystone, revered for affordable shows, beer and solid cocktails. If you're hungry after, head next door to Bite Café, a diner with a BYO policy under the same ownership.

ANDY'S JAZZ CLUB
11 East Hubbard Street (between North State and North Wabash), +1 312 642 6805, andysjazzclub.com
open daily

EMPTY BOTTLE
1035 North Western Avenue (between West Thomas and West Cortez), +1 773 276 3600, emptybottle.com
open daily

THE ANNOYANCE THEATRE & BAR
851 West Belmont Avenue (between North Clark and North Sheffield), +1 773 697 9693, theannoyance.com
open daily

THE GREEN MILL
4802 North Broadway Street (between West Lawrence and West Gunnison), +1 773 878 5552
greenmilljazz.com, open daily

THE HIDEOUT
1354 West Wabansia Avenue (between North Throop and North Ada), +1 773 227 4433, hideoutchicago.com
open daily

THE iO THEATER
1501 North Kingsbury Street (between West Blackhawk and West Weed), +1 312 929 2401, ioimprov.com
open daily

As evidenced by the laundry list of comedic talents to come out of Chicago, this city is a breeding ground for improv artists. Though Second City is a staple, a better bet might be improv at **The iO Theater**. Here, the audience gets up close and awkwardly personal with the cast performances. It's an exhilarating ride to witness up-and-coming comics whir through spontaneous skits with such hilarious dexterity.

The most enjoyable comedy show I've ever seen was a satirical riff on the classic video game, *The Oregon Trail*. It was a nostalgic, uproarious masterpiece at **The Annoyance Theatre & Bar**. Such quirkiness is par for the course here. In a city with such an ample live comedy scene, it's impressive when an underdog theater such as this really raises the bar.

Tucked in the middle of a quiet warehouse district near Lincoln Park, **The Hideout** is one of the most unexpected late night surprises in town. The cabin-looking bar draws an incredibly wide array of talents from its musical performances to its recurring Soup & Bread nights to veggie bingo events. Yes, this is a bar that hosts bingo with bushels of produce as prizes. Dreams do come true, kids.

CHICAGO AFTER DARK:
booze it up

Where to throw 'em back

Chicago loves its liquor. Every which way you turn, in any part of the city, you'll find a variety of watering holes. From elevated cocktail bars and classic dives to craft beer bastions, Chicago has them all.

It's classic meets contemporary at **The California Clipper**, one of the city's most iconic drinking dens. A longtime Humboldt Park haunt for cheap drinks in a dark, lounge-y environment, the bar underwent rejuvenation under new ownership in 2014. Now, the same ethos is intact while the drink list has expanded to encyclopedic lengths. Everything from boozy ice cream to Sazeracs are available to be comfortably enjoyed under the crimson glow of this windowless hideaway.

THE CALIFORNIA CLIPPER

Named after a Prohibition-era American evangelist, **Billy Sunday** is one of the craftier cocktail bars in bar-happy Logan Square. The meticulous drink list changes regularly, featuring thoughtful – and aesthetically pleasing – drinks that run the gamut from black aloe quaffs to shareable elixirs served in carved pumpkins.

In terms of dive bars, you'd be hard pressed to find a more reliable staple than Pilsen's **Skylark**. Expansive, loud and properly dingy, Skylark sports a bit of a manic basement feel. But the cheery service belies the derelict façade, as does the highly affordable craft beer selection and the pierogies, perfect for sopping up a long night of boozing.

A bit farther south, you'll find Bridgeport's beer darling: **Maria's Packaged Goods & Community Bar**. Part liquor store, part upscale neighborhood watering hole, Maria's is a family-run institution with one of the most impressive beer selections in any Chicago bar.

If it's a raucous night you're after, here's what to do: hit up a convenience store and stock up on gummy candy to BYO to **Alice's Lounge** in Avondale. Nosh on said candy, chug some cheap beer and rack up the nerve to perform karaoke. If you're feeling saucy, follow Alice's up with some dancing at nearby Late Bar.

While it doesn't have karaoke, **Vera** offers up expert Spanish fare. This wine bar is one of the top drinking and dining nooks in the city, presided over by the ever so lovely husband-wife duo Mark and Liz Mendez. And boy do they know what they're doing, serving up a masterful wine program (with a thoughtful ode to sherry, no less) to accent the irresistible snacks.

ALICE'S LOUNGE
3556 West Belmont Avenue (between North Central Park and North Drake), +1 773 279 9382 facebook.com/pages/Alices-Lounge, closed Sunday

BILLY SUNDAY
3143 West Logan Boulevard (between North Kedzie and North Milwaukee), +1 773 661 2485 billy-sunday.com, open daily

MARIA'S PACKAGED GOODS & COMMUNITY BAR
960 West 31st Street (across from South Morgan Street), +1 773 890 0588, community-bar.com open daily

SKYLARK
2149 South Halsted Street (between West 21st and West Cermak), +1 312 948 5275, skylarkchicago.com open daily

THE CALIFORNIA CLIPPER
1002 North California Avenue (between West Augusta and West Cortez), +1 773 384 2547 californiaclipper.com, open daily

VERA
1023 West Lake Street (between North Carpenter and North Morgan), +1 312 243 9770, verachicago.com open daily

river north

Every city has one: the shiny, loud, people-packed neighborhood swelling with tourist sights, shops, nightlife venues, restaurants and bars. Here in Chicago, the honor belongs to River North. The most congested of the downtown 'hoods, this is an area flooded with entertainment options on every corner. It's a taste of Chicago at its most illustrious, where crowds comprise an all-inclusive range of sports fans, hipsters, glitterati, celebrities, families, students and everything in between. A metropolitan melting pot of cultures, River North bursts with all the sights and sounds that are indicative of true city life: stunning art galleries, storied steakhouses, upscale cocktail bars, niche musuems and bakeries whose goods are worth the wait.

DOUGHNUT VAULT

Piping-hot deliciousness

401 North Franklin Street (between West Kinzie and West Hubbard)
No phone / doughnutvault.com / Open daily

Here's how it's gonna go: you're going to set your alarm, head downtown and throw elbows if you need to in order to arrive at Doughnut Vault first. Since opening day in 2011, this shoebox-sized breakfast counter sees queues down the street on a daily basis. Rain or shine, humid or frigid, people arrive in droves to check out the end all-be all of doughnut shops. One bite and you'll see why. My first taste of the tire-sized chocolate glazed yeast confection stopped me dead in my tracks. Ditto the impeccable buttermilk old-fashioned, glistening with treacly glaze. It's stupefying how any ring of dough could be so perfect. Doughnut Vault does one thing and it does it very well. Brave the lines and you'll agree.

GENE & GEORGETTI

Throwback steakhouse

500 North Franklin Street (between West Illinois and West Grand)
+1 312 527 3718 / geneandgeorgetti.com / Closed Sunday

The first time I patronized Gene & Georgetti, I looked around the dining room and saw older couples conversing with the wait staff like old friends. Everyone looked like they'd been regulars for decades. That's par for the course at this longstanding restaurant, in business since 1941. It's as much about the enduring community as it is about the hulking portions of steaks and seafood. In a neighborhood as hyper-modern as River North, it's a meaty breath of fresh air to visit a place as preserved as Gene & Georgetti. Sip on a soup bowl-sized glass of red, pair it with an expertly prepared New York strip and join the crowd.

HEADQUARTERS BEERCADE

Pints and video games

213 West Institute Place (between North Franklin and North Wells)
+1 312 291 8735 / hqbeercade.com / Open daily

Like many kids of my generation, arcades were my jam. Some of my fondest memories revolve around pinball and beating the X-Men and Simpsons games. When I grew up, I pretty much resigned myself to being done with the gaming palaces. Then a curious thing happened: adult arcades, complete with bars, became a thing in Chicago, and from the onslaught came this almighty temple of liquored nostalgia. Located in a refurbished warehouse space, Headquarters Beercade sports a wide array of free game machines, from my beloved pinball to retro *NBA Jam* to racing and shooting games. What makes it even better? Craft cocktails, beer and a DJ booth. It's a far cry from the arcades of my youth, but a welcome update, indeed.

MAYA POLSKY GALLERY

Art in all its forms

215 West Superior Street (between North Wells and North Franklin)
+1 312 440 0055 / mayapolskygallery.com / **Closed Sunday**
and Monday

In Chicago's expansive, immersive gallery district, Maya Polsky Gallery has
been holding it down for decades. In business since 1989, this art space
is second to none. Exhibits are rotated on a regular basis, keeping things
fresh, exciting and novel. Contemporary art is at the crux of things here,
depicted in works focused on the likes of history, nature, the environment
and gender, realized through sculpture, print and painting. These are all
familiar, relatable facets of humanity, and it's fascinating to view them
through such a multifaceted lens.

MUSEUM OF BROADCAST COMMUNICATIONS

Homage to radio and television

360 North State Street (between West Kinzie and the Chicago River)
+1 312 245 8200 / museum.tv / Closed Sunday and Monday

If you're looking for something a little different – or are a pop culture fanatic – don't miss the Museum of Broadcast Communications. With a sense of whimsy, humor and engagement, this museum transcends generations. Paraphernalia from Oprah's former Chicago TV studio is on hand, as are the sets from *Meet the Press* and local news stations. But TV isn't the star of the show: the llustrious Radio Hall of Fame whose diverse inductees include Abbott and Costello, Dick Clark, Ira Glass, Orson Welles, Terry Gross and Wendy Williams is housed here. Special exhibits are often nostalgic, like the *Salute to America's Greatest Icons*, which featured characters like Rice Krispy's Snap, Crackle and Pop and ensured that museum guests didn't leave without a Rice Krispy treat. Definitely my kind of museum.

P.O.S.H.

Vintage home décor finds

613 North State Street (between East Ohio and East Ontario)
+1 312 280 1602 / poshchicago.com / Open daily

There's really only one way to feel when entering a shop called P.O.S.H. and that feeling is – you guessed it – posh. Case in point: The first time I walked into this home goods shop, I felt the need to purchase an antique silver spoon and create an entire dinner party around it. The place is designed to help you up your entertaining game with Champagne glass sets, cocktail stirrers and heavy drawers packed with mismatched silver and platters. If I were an Anglophile or Francophile, I'd buy every map and coronation brooch in the store. But I'll just stick to collecting an assortment of functional items like the sleekest feather duster I've ever seen, and of course, silver spoons for ritzy dinner parties.

THE BERKSHIRE ROOM

Raising the bar on hotel bars

1st Floor ACME Hotel Company, 15 East Ohio Street (between North State and North Wabash) / +1 312 894 0945 / theberkshireroom.com Open daily

I am desperately trying to make The Berkshire Room my personal Cheers. Only one obstacle stands in my way: this glamorous establishment, tucked in the back of ACME Hotel Company (see pg 5), is much too popular and perpetually crowded for me to stand out. Nevertheless, I'm magnetized by this chic pub, a dark and romantic den of intimate corners, anchored by a massive, shiny bar with Benjamin Schiller overseeing a masterful drink list. The dexterous Schiller shakes up a host of beautiful tipples, but I suggest you try one of his barrel-aged cocktails and snack on some bourbon-cured olives: you'll soon see why I'm obsessed with the place.

THE GOLDEN TRIANGLE

Worldly housewares

330 North Clark Street (between West Kinzie and the Chicago River)
+1 312 755 1266 / **goldentriangle.biz** / **Closed Sunday**

The first thing you need to know before entering The Golden Triangle is that it's not your average furniture store. The shop originated as a Thai artifacts outlet in 1989, but over the years, the massive warehouse space has ballooned to include vintage and modern finds from throughout Asia, Europe and right here in Chicago. The sprawling space, comprised of a labyrinthine layout of themed rooms, feels more like an inspiring museum than anything. Unlike museums, you can actually purchase everything you see before you. The Golden Triangle's multifaceted inventory, displayed in transportive rooms that take you to China, England and beyond, smartly melds the new with the antiquated. Be careful though, it's dangerously tempting to spend rent money here.

THREE DOTS AND A DASH

An underground world of tropical wonders

435 North Clark Street (between West Hubbard and West Illinois)
+1 312 610 4220 / threedotschicago.com / Open daily

Few places sport the wow factor that tiki-inspired Three Dots and a Dash does. Hands down, it's the number one place I take out-of-towners when they visit. From those first steps through the doors to the final sips of your last cocktail, it's a thoroughly fun and memorable experience. The clandestine bar is accessed through a blue-lit alley, down a set of stairs illuminated by a wall of glowing skulls. The whole thing is very *Pirates of the Caribbean*, doing a handy job of transporting guests out of Chicago and onto a tropical island. Servers wear leis, pupu platters brim with coconut shrimp and cocktails pack a punch. Everyone from my dad to my friends from NYC is hooked by this subterranean wonderland of boozy pleasures.

XOCO

Mexican street food with style

449 North Clark Street (between West Hubbard and West Illinois)
No phone / rickbayless.com/restaurants/xoco
Closed Sunday and Monday

At a cursory glance, churros, tortas and caldos seem like humble creations.
Why, then, the insatiable crowds flocking to XOCO? It helps to have Rick Bayless,
a demigod of a chef in the modern Mexican arena, behind the brand. While the
more upscale Topolobampo and Frontera Grill are on the same block, this casual
endeavor is all about Mexican street food, made with considerable panache by
the *Top Chef Masters* victor. The wood-fired tortas, made with crusty bread and
laden with locally sourced meats and vegetables, are phenomenal, and the soups
(caldos) are life-affirming, especially the avocado-packed vegetable variety.
Don't miss the churros, twisted into an ichthus shape, glazed with the likes of
pistachio and hazelnut and ideally dunked in thick Mexican drinking chocolate.

RPM STEAK

a cut above

Chicago's swankiest steakhouses

CHICAGO CUT STEAKHOUSE
300 North LaSalle Street (between the
Chicago River and West Kinzie), +1 312 329 1800
chicagocutsteakhouse.com, open daily

GIBSONS BAR & STEAKHOUSE
1028 North Rush Street (between North State and East
Bellevue), +1 312 266 8999, gibsonssteakhouse.com
open daily

KINZIE CHOPHOUSE
400 North Wells Street (between West Kinzie and
West Hubbard), +1 312 822 0191, kinziechophouse.com
open daily

PRIME & PROVISIONS
222 North LaSalle Street (between West Upper
Wacker and West Lake), +1 312 726 7777
primeandprovisions.com, open daily

RPM STEAK
66 West Kinzie Street (between North Dearborn and
North Clark), +1 312 284 4990, rpmsteak.com
open daily

Nestled in the heartland of America, surrounded by farms, it's really no
surprise that Chicagoans like beef and take their steakhouses seriously.
Some in the city are mainstays that date back to Al Capone's days (the man
was a ruffian, but he sure had good taste!), while slick newcomers draw in
crowds from all over.

I've already told you about the legendary Gene & Georgetti (see pg 79); another staple, **Kinzie Chophouse**, sits two blocks away, tucked under the "L". Once through the doors, bask in the radiant jazz tunes and the wafting aroma of jumbo baked potatoes. The menu is massive, but steaks are king, available in every cut and preparation, from Oscar-style with crabmeat to peppercorn-crusted or blackened with Cajun seasoning.

If it's a scene you're looking for, you'll find it at **Gibsons Bar & Steakhouse**. The walls here are lined with framed celebrity memorabilia and filled with moneyed clientele who look like they could buy the entire block without blinking. The bacon-packed wedge salad and Alaskan crab claws are tempting, but save room for the gargantuan steaks and chops, plus slices of cake and pie as big as my torso.

Though new, **Chicago Cut Steakhouse** looks to be a legend in the making. Not only are the riverside views unparalleled, but the innovative wine list and USDA prime beef fixin's are good enough to entice the likes of Beyoncé and Barack Obama. If it's good enough for them...

Prime & Provisions is another hot new contender. While much of the Loop used to get sleepy after business hours, places like this have convinced downtowners to stick around, luring them in with the promise of the highest quality Kansas-sourced Black Angus beef, classic cocktails shaken to a tee and a menu of premium cigars from all over the world. The restaurant even has its own signature blended cigar, dubbed "Provisiones".

Then there's **RPM Steak**. This glitzy, chef-centric River North spot raises the bar by rounding out its menu with the likes of miso-roasted Maine lobster, coal-roasted chicken and seared foie gras served with seasonal fruit. It's a bit of a throwback to the olden days of steakhouse pomp and circumstance, with servers clad in tuxedos pricier than my rent and steaks so large they could feed a family.

west loop

Home to Restaurant Row, Fulton Market District and Oprah Winfrey's bygone Harpo Studios, the West Loop is, unquestionably, the best Loop (in case you were wondering, the Loop is made up of three sections: the North, West and South Loops). Lined with some of the country's most delicious restaurants, most classic markets and warehouses aplenty, this neighborhood offers a curious mix of modern and olden. On any given block, a hot new bar shares sidewalk space with a fishmonger. A glossy Google office overlooks a defunct train depot. Stiletto-clad fashionistas cross paths with butchers, bakers and probably even candlestick-makers. There's plenty to see and do when Chicago history melds with present-day.

1   Au Cheval
2   avec
3   Chicago French
     Market
4   Girl & the Goat
5   J.P. Graziano Grocery
     Co., Inc.
6   RM Champagne Salon
7   TÊTE Charcuterie
8   The Aviary
9   The Publican
10 Tribeca

AU CHEVAL

Creative interpretations of classic diner fare

800 West Randolph Street (at North Halsted) / +1 312 929 4580
auchevalchicago.com / Open daily

One of my good friends spent the majority of her life as a vegetarian. When eventually the craving for meat became inescapable, she (correctly) decided the best place to leap off the wagon was Au Cheval. Specifically, she wanted their cheeseburger. Not just any cheeseburger; this double patty burger (a "single" comes with two patties and a "double" with three) arrives smothered in dijonnaise, cheese, pickles and an optional egg, all topped on a perfectly crusty bun. I suspect many a vegetarian has been derailed by the undeniable pleasures of this dimly lit, perpetually packed neo-diner where that acclaimed burger shares menu space with fried bologna sandwiches and scrambled eggs with foie gras. With food this indulgent and salacious, it's easy to see why.

AVEC

Mediterranean small plates and wine

615 West Randolph Street (between North Jefferson and North Desplaines) / +1 312 377 2002 / avecrestaurant.com / Open daily

You're a predictable Chicagoan if you cite avec as your favorite place to dine. And yet, year after year, I give it a spot among my top five. Who could deny the pleasure of sitting inside a restaurant that looks like a sauna (especially during the winter months), tucking into half carafes of wine and the most addictive chorizo-stuffed bacon-wrapped Medjool dates? Here's how I do avec: start with the aforementioned wine and dates. If I'm starving, I throw in an order of creamy brandade with the tallegio focaccia, then add more wine and call it a night. Occasionally I'll add a virtuous dish of greens or even go out of my comfort zone with one of the weekly specials. But really, when the staples are this great, why mess with a good thing?

CHICAGO FRENCH MARKET

Vive la France!

131 North Clinton Street (between West Randolph and West Washington) / **+1 312 575 0306** / **frenchmarketchicago.com**
Closed Sunday

San Francisco has its Ferry Building. Seattle has its Pike Place Market. And Chicago has its French Market. This year-round European-style market is packed with a plethora of vendors slinging their artisanal wares from inside the bustling Ogilvie Transportation Center. Perfect for train commuters, the lively food fair is the ideal spot to binge on everything from baguettes and cheeses to bánh mì, doughnuts and frites. In between bites, do some grocery shopping for smoked meats at Fumare, produce at City Fresh and bouquets from Les Fleurs. Whether dining in for lunch or stockpiling dinner ingredients, this is the market to visit. Now to figure out how to carry the bounty onto the train...

GIRL & THE GOAT

Seasonal small plates

809 West Randolph Street (between North Halsted and North Green)
+1 312 492 6262 / girlandthegoat.com / Open daily

Ever since her win on *Top Chef*, Stephanie Izard has been a darling in the food world, and the consistent crowd at Girl & the Goat is a testament to her fan base. Her food combines some of the most surprising flavors you'll find in town. You'd never bet on grapefruit pairing well with lentils and sunchokes, or tempura fish with bacon sweet 'n' sour, but, not only do the flavor combinations exceed expectations, they pair well with both the local 3 Floyds beer on tap and the house wine. And, of course, there's always at least one dish featuring goat. Don't let the crowds scare you if you don't have a reservation: find room at the bar, where the entire menu is available.

J.P. GRAZIANO GROCERY CO., INC.

Go old-school on Restaurant Row

901 West Randolph Street (at North Peoria) / +1 312 666 4587
jpgraziano.com / Closed Sunday

J.P. Graziano Grocery might well be located on one of the hottest strips of dining real estate in the city, but it more than holds its own as a bastion of bygone comfort amidst a sea of modern, expensive restaurants. Whereas most spots in the area necessitate trading a kidney in order to get a reservation, this place is as welcoming and familial as it's been since it opened in the 1930s. Jim Graziano keeps the family business alive and well, operating like a well-oiled machine (olive oil, naturally) building Italian subs for the lunch rush and stocking provisions from the homeland. Once you're done filling your grocery basket and your belly, don't neglect to snag a cannoli to go.

RM CHAMPAGNE SALON

French delights in a dark alley

116 North Green Street (between West Randolph and West Washington) / **+1 312 243 1199** / **rmchampagnesalon.com** / **Open daily**

As a general rule, I don't wander down alleyways. Common sense tells me these dark, narrow lanes are filled with dumpsters and potential crime; but in the case of the Green Street alley, home to RM Champagne Salon, I am dead wrong. Tucked discreetly down a cobblestone-lined alleyway, RM is a romantic little slice of Paris in Chicago. Twinkly lights illuminate a gorgeous courtyard, while the interior, with its open fire, makes me feel like I've stumbled into the fantastical restaurant from *Ratatouille*. Champagne is, of course, the name of the game at this gorgeous parlor, and is available in all sizes and price points. When paired with oysters, champignon flatbread and cassoulet, this place reaches a new level of magnifique altogether.

TÊTE CHARCUTERIE

Homage to the city's meat-packing district

1114 West Randolph Street (between North Aberdeen and North May) / **+1 312 733 1178** / **tetechicago.com** / **Closed Sunday**

Chicago has a storied history as an industrial town. While the unsavory practices uncovered in Upton Sinclair's famously grisly novel, *The Jungle*, are a thing of the past, this city's love of meat remains firmly intact. TÊTE Charcuterie celebrates this love, big time. The entrancing restaurant, outfitted with an open kitchen, provides a front-row view of the chefs cooking up a storm with locally sourced ingredients, including offal, which they utilize in all sorts of ways — from German-inspired sausages to pepperoni snack sticks and maple-cured duck rillettes. Don't overlook the meticulous vegetable preparations either, like a beet salad with pistachio-goat cheese nougat or shishito peppers with black bean aioli. TÊTE does Midwestern cuisine loud and proud.

THE AVIARY

Cocktail bar, redefined

955 West Fulton Market (at North Morgan) / +1 312 226 0868
theaviary.com / Closed Monday and Tuesday

Chef and proprietor Grant Achatz receives most of the accolades when it comes to praising this innovative bar, but after spending a day with his glassware designer, Martin Kastner, it's hard not to think Achatz's counterpart deserves as much attention. While we typically go to a bar to drink, here the sipping experience is as much about presentation as it is about taste. For example, one cocktail comes in a vacuum-pot coffee brewer and another is served in a porthole-style flattened teapot. You'll probably want to take a serving glass to go, but unless you've spent your month's paycheck on drinks, you'll be sober enough to know that's not an option.

THE PUBLICAN

Fine pork, beer and oysters

837 West Fulton Market (at North Green) / **+1 312 733 9555**
thepublicanrestaurant.com / **Open daily**

There are few instances when I actually enjoy feeling like part of a cattle call. Boarding a plane is not one of them; dining at The Publican is. Scoring one of the wooden booths enclosed with swinging doors at this Fulton Market beer hall means you've snagged one of the most coveted spots to dine in the West Loop: surrounded by a standing crowd throwing back beers in the nearby bar area, and next to communal diners grappling over food and drinks. Oyster- and beer-lovers are in luck, but for those after my own heart, find a friend and share the mussels and a roasted half chicken – one of the best poultry preparations in town.

TRIBECA

The West Loop's style icon

1035 West Madison Street (between South Aberdeen and South Morgan) / **+1 312 492 9373** / **shopattribeca.com** / **Open daily**

When a boutique receives new shipments of clothes from the coasts at the same level of frequency that a sushi chef sources fish, you know you're shopping in the right place. Tribeca has been styling the West Loop for upwards of two decades, long before the downtown neighborhood was the fashion hotbed it is today. While Chicago has never been on the same level as cities like New York or Los Angeles when it comes to sartorial offerings, Tribeca helps give our Midwestern metropolis the cred it deserves. This slick women's boutique offers a little bit of everything, from flowery day dresses to cocktail party attire, vacation garb and chunky, eye-catching accessories that look like they'd be right at home on an Olsen.

CINDY'S

If cities had height requirements, Chicago would easily be tall enough to enter (and dominate) the NBA. The birthplace of the modern skyscraper, Chicago is all about altitude, as evidenced by our immaculate skyline and the array of rooftop destinations.

At Harold Washington Library, the city's primary – and largest – public library, lives a majestic atrium called the **Winter Garden**. Once you traverse your way through the labyrinthine library up to the ninth floor, you'll enter this glass-domed beauty that bursts with greenery and is awash with natural light. A modest array of small tables scattered throughout the huge space makes for a fine location to sit down and read or work on your laptop. The supreme tranquility up here does wonders for the mind.

One of the most gorgeous terraces in Chicago, the sprawling patio at **Terrace at Trump** sports wraparound views of River North, the Wrigley Building, the Chicago River, Lake Michigan and the Loop. There's plenty to admire between sips of elegant cocktails and bites of strawberry shortcake.

Perched atop the recently renovated Chicago Athletic Association Hotel (see pg 6), **Cindy's** is one of the hottest tickets in the Loop. The 13th-floor rooftop bar and terrace overlooks Millennium Park, providing an illustrious backdrop for shareable contemporary American plates and haute cocktails.

Away from the splashiness a little bit, one of my favorite rooftop gems is **Drumbar**, which sits on top of the Raffaello Hotel. Located on the 18th floor, utterly surrounded

CINDY'S
13th Floor Chicago Athletic Association Hotel, 12 South
Michigan Avenue (between East Madison
and East Monroe), +1 312 792 3502
chicagoathletichotel.com, open daily

DRUMBAR
18th Floor Raffaello Hotel, 201 East Delaware Place
(between Mies van der Rohe and North Dewitt)
+1 312 933 4805, drumbar.com, open daily

I|O GODFREY
127 West Huron Street (between North LaSalle and
North Clark), +1 312 374 1830, iogodfrey.com, open daily

TERRACE AT TRUMP
401 North Wabash Avenue (between West Kinzie and
the Chicago River), +1 312 588 8600
trumphotelcollection.com/chicago/rooftop-
restaurants-chicago.php, open daily

WINTER GARDEN
9th Floor Harold Washington Library, 400 South State
Street (between East Van Buren and West Congress),
+1 312 747 4300, chipublib.org, open daily

by urban jungle, this place takes its cocktails seriously, boasting one of the more elaborate and impressive drink lists around. The outdoor deck has the feel of a dignified garden party, while the interior is just as exciting with a motif that looks like it could be a room in *Clue*.

While Chicago may be chock-full of rooftop bars, very few of them are accessible year round thanks to that pesky thing called winter. But with its enormous retractable roof – the largest in town – **I|O Godfrey** is one of the few rooftop spaces in Chicago open through all the seasons. The massive retractable glass roof provides a front-row seat to the downtown skyline, and the kitchen-crafted cocktails, a roaring fire pit, two bar areas and imaginative American cuisine will have you daydreaming of moving in.

pilsen

Walking down 18th Street, through the heart of Pilsen amid a flurry of colorful culture, feels like exploring the inside of a piñata. It's a place where Mexican culture and art collide in all sorts of ways. This is immediately evident upon stepping off the 18th Street train platform, where murals line the station and provide the gateway to a neighborhood full of bright visuals and cultural experiences. The eclectic, energetic southwest side area is a long standing enclave for Mexican expats — and is one of the largest Mexican populations in the US — evident in its surfeit of tortillerias, carnitas shops and bodegas. Nowhere else do generations-old Mexican businesses weave together so seamlessly as in Pilsen, where vintage stores, modern bars and restaurants, art galleries and hip coffee shops share real estate with the long-established vibrancy of the neighborhood's roots.

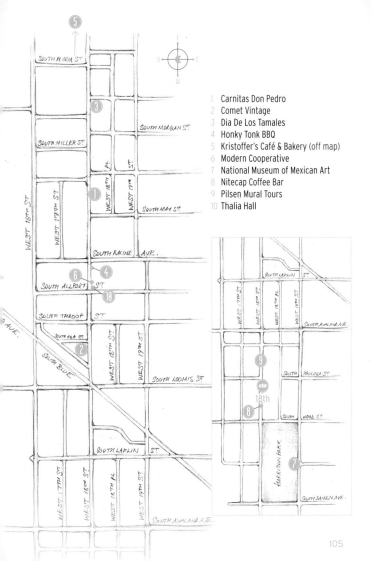

1   Carnitas Don Pedro
2   Comet Vintage
3   Dia De Los Tamales
4   Honky Tonk BBQ
5   Kristoffer's Café & Bakery (off map)
6   Modern Cooperative
7   National Museum of Mexican Art
8   Nitecap Coffee Bar
9   Pilsen Mural Tours
10   Thalia Hall

CARNITAS DON PEDRO

Pig out on Mexican pork

1113 West 18th Street (between South May and South Carpenter)
+1 312 829 4757 / **facebook.com/pages/Don-Pedro-Carnitas**
Open daily

Vegetarians, be warned. Pork is king at Carnitas Don Pedro, a dive-y hole-in-the-wall along Pilsen's main artery. On a daily basis, people line up for the luscious carnitas with the same committed fervor of shoppers on Black Friday. Upon entry, you'll see unabashed mounds of glistening pork in every iteration, from their fatty namesake to crispy chicharrones and even more unusual, unnerving items like pig brain. Like I said, not the place for herbivores. You can order pork by the pound for use at home, like many regulars do, or you can stuff your face with carnitas tacos served simply with warm tortillas, cilantro and onions.

COMET VINTAGE

Apparel that is out of this world

1320 West 18th Street (at South Ada)   +1 312 733 7327
cometvintagechicago.com   Open daily

Walking into Comet Vintage for the first time, I felt the same kind of awe that Ariel from *The Little Mermaid* surely felt when she discovered a whole new world on land. A fascinating, eclectic array of accessories, clothing and accoutrements line every inch of this funky little shop that constantly rotates their inventory to offer something new every time I visit. I marvel at the hats, obsess over the ties, waft in the scent of the candles and wish I wore contacts so that I wouldn't be blind modeling their chic sunglasses.

DIA DE LOS TAMALES

A revolutionary take on a classic

939 West 18th Street (between South Sangamon and South Morgan)
+1 312 496 3057 / diadelostamales.com / Open daily

When I first sampled the fare from Dia De Los Tamales it became immediately apparent this was a far cry from the traditional masa snacks I tend to scarf from street vendors late at night. Rather, tamales peddled at this slick Mexican restaurant come from a chef-driven standpoint. This makes for an menu packed with fusion tamales, such as coconut curry chicken, Cuban pork, Buffalo chicken, Chicago beef and even dessert offerings like apple cobbler and chocolate-peanut butter. Each one is rich, hearty and filling, lending new depth of flavor and texture to the typical tamale tradition.

HONKY TONK BBQ

Southern eats on the southwest side

1800 South Racine Avenue (at 18th Street) / **+1 312 226 7427**
honkytonkbbqchicago.com / **Closed Monday**

A good barbecue joint shouldn't feel like a formulaic dining experience;
it should take you to a boisterous setting bursting with music, good
vibes and smoky meats. That's precisely what Honky Tonk BBQ does.
The award-winning haunt feels more like a backyard cookout than a
restaurant, complete with live tunes, late-night grub and wood-fired
barbecue. All the succulent requisites are accounted for: pulled pork, ribs,
brisket and smoked chicken. While those are yummy and well-worth
ordering, don't sleep on the less common items, like corn-filled empanadas,
the fried green tomato BLT, bourbon-soaked pound cake and bacon "candy".
As the name hints, Honky Tonk is a place that's as fun as it is flavorful.

KRISTOFFER'S CAFÉ & BAKERY

Coffee with a side of tres leches

1733 South Halsted Street (between West 17th and West 18th)
+1 312 829 4150 / facebook.com/Kristoffers-Cafe-Bakery
Closed Monday

When Rick Bayless, the godfather of haute Mexican cuisine, endorses a piece of tres leches cake, you take heed. The aforementioned cake is found at Pilsen's Kristoffer's Cafe & Bakery, a welcoming coffee shop and dessert retreat that will have you instantly falling in café love. It's the kind of warm nook you can easily hole up in for hours, whether you're reading your way through a book or working away on a computer. And while the menu includes coffee as well as savory selections like tamales and quesadillas, you're really here for the incomparable desserts. The many varieties of tres leches are rightfully esteemed, as is the almighty "chocoflan", a novel hybrid of chocolate cake and flan perfection.

MODERN COOPERATIVE

Antique chic

1215 West 18th Street (between South Racine and South Allport)
+1 312 226 8525 / **moderncooperative.com** / **Open daily**

Boasting a huge amount of vintage goods that span furniture, wall fixtures and apparel, Modern Cooperative has a bit of everything to satisfy the dreams of home décor junkies. The enormous space inside Thalia Hall (see pg 115) feels like raiding an aristocrat's palatial attic, where antiques juxtapose modern furnishings and decorative archery equipment is on hand alongside stylish hats and photography paraphernalia. Many of the items come from local artists who specialize in repurposing materials, while the owners scour other items on antiquing trips. Whether you're looking to splurge on a new dining room set or pick up an unconventional paperweight, you'll find what you're after at Modern Cooperative.

IMMIGRANT IDENTIFICATION CARD
UNITED STATES
DEPARTMENT OF LABOR

SURNAME

GIVEN NAME

COUNTRY OF BIRTH   DATE OF BIRTH

NATIONALITY   COLOR OF EYES

PORT OF ARRIVAL   STEAMSHIP

DATE ADMITTED   STATUS OF ADMISSION

IMMIGRANT'S SIGNATURE

IMMIGRANT INSPECTOR

NATIONAL MUSEUM OF MEXICAN ART

A dose of culture from Mexico

1852 West 19th Street (between South Wood and South Wolcott)
+1 312 738 1503 / nationalmuseumofmexicanart.org / Closed Monday

As evidenced by the neighborhood-wide mélange of world-famous murals, art is paramount in Mexican culture. It all comes together in magnificent unison at the National Museum of Mexican Art, an exploratory destination with upwards of 7,500 art pieces and room after room of lustrous displays, ranging from quirky to thought-provoking. Everything from traditional garb to the plight of immigrants is on display; on my most recent visit, new exhibitions included a community-oriented area called *The House on Mango Street*, after the Sandra Cisneros novel of the same name, and another complex space dubbed Deportable Aliens. As I left, I couldn't help but smile underneath the pink-lit sign, "Make Tacos Not War." Amen.

NITECAP COFFEE BAR

Caffeine plus community

1738 West 18th Street (between South Wood and South Paulina)
+1 312 846 1149 / nitecapcoffee.com / Open daily

When I'm drinking my daily cup of coffee, I often think to myself, "Man, I wish my tarot cards were being read right now." Or "Gee, why can't I also be watching *Beetlejuice* at this very moment?" The stars align at Nitecap Coffee Bar, a café that is so much more than your standard java joint. Established with a community gathering mindset, the coffee shop features a resident tarot card reader, Laura, along with movie nights and live jazz. Even the regular furnishings are outré, from a small bed dangling from the wall to a mural of the Chicago skyline designed with coffee cups. The menu is solid as well, featuring local coffee roasters and snacks like red wine cookies.

PILSEN MURAL TOURS

Street art to behold

1634 West 18th Street (between South Marshfield and South Paulina)
+1 708 557 5400 / walkchicagotours.com/tours/pilsen.html
Open daily

Few places in the world can hold a candle to the dynamic murals
displayed across Pilsen's walls. Far beyond your standard bill of graffiti,
the works here are museum-caliber creations that run the gamut from
The Muppets to Quetzalcoatl and the Stork. These were in part commissioned
by the Chicago Urban Art Society, which enticed such street artists as
Juan Angel Chavez and Jeff Zimmerman to conceptualize murals depicting
the cultures and character of the neighborhood. Walk Chicago Tours curates
organized routes to get you up close and personal, but if you're interested
in exploring on your own, the best murals are bounded by Halsted Street,
16th Street and Western Avenue.

THALIA HALL

Historic landmark, modern style

1807 South Allport Street (at 18th Street) / **+1 312 526 3851**
thaliahallchicago.com / **Open daily**

Not every concert hall boasts a beer-oriented restaurant, a punch bar
and a saloon. Nor is every concert hall a century-old public hall-turned-
city mainstay. Thalia Hall is far from average; it's an enduring palace
of a venue, originally commissioned as a community hall in 1892 by
John Dusek. Today, his community-focused dream lives on in new ways.
The hall serves as a venue for a miscellany of indie music acts and events,
the ground floor operates as a decadent restaurant named Dusek's Board
and Beer, and Punch House comprises the basement, a '70s-esque bar
complete with jelly cocktails, boozy snow cones, a glowing fish tank and
a rotating bookcase door. New addition Tack Room, a saloon-y piano bar,
aptly takes up the old carriage house.

hyde park

History pulses through the lifeblood of
Hyde Park, a neighborhood situated on Chicago's
south side along the shores of Lake Michigan.
From a university campus that could pass as
Hogwarts to a thriving jazz and gospel music scene
and a museum born from the remnants of the
World's Columbian Exposition, this is an area deeply
entrenched in its roots. Stone manors, renowned
architecture, expansive boulevards and even
President Obama's Chicago home can be found (and
marveled at) in Hyde Park, which feels worlds away
from downtown even though it's a quick drive down
Lake Shore. From the co-op bookstores to the hip new
haunts, it's a neighborhood perfect for getting lost
and getting inspired.

1   57th Street Books
2   Encore
3   Frederick C. Robie House
4   Hyde Park Records
5   Osaka Garden

6   The Oriental Institute Museum
     of the University of Chicago
7   The Promontory
8   Valois

EAST HYDE PARK BLVD.

EAST 52ND ST.

51st/53rd St
(Hyde Park)

EAST 53RD ST.

SOUTH HARPER AVE.

SOUTH UNIVERSITY AVE.
SOUTH WOODLAWN AVE.
SOUTH KIMBARK AVE.
SOUTH KENWOOD AVE.
SOUTH DORCHESTER AVE.
SOUTH BLACKSTONE AVE.

SOUTH CORNELL AVE.
SOUTH HYDE PARK BLVD.

EAST 55TH ST.

55th/56th/57th St

EAST 56TH ST.

JACKSON PARK

EAST 57TH ST.

EAST 58TH ST.

59th St (University
of Chicago)

EAST 59TH ST.

MIDWAY PLAISANCE
EAST 60TH ST.

WEST LAGOON

EAST LAGOON

57TH STREET BOOKS

Step away from the Kindle

1301 East 57th Street (at South Kimbark) / **+1 773 684 1300**
semcoop.com / **Open daily**

No offense to technology, but e-books will never capture the age-old sensation of flipping through a good book, dog-earing the pages and breathing in that ink-and-paper aroma. Part of the Seminary Co-op Bookstores collective, a duo of shops in Hyde Park owned by members since 1961, 57th Street Books is nestled below street level; a low-ceilinged legend that feels like the best kind of funky basement. Row after row of shelves filled with every imaginable literary genre and style snake through an immense space that's dotted with little nooks and crannies for reading. With that precious scent of timeworn paper wafting through the air, this is an Eden for bibliophiles like me.

ENCORE

Clothing with a purpose

1553 East Hyde Park Boulevard (at South Cornell) / +1 773 324 1111
facebook.com/Encore-Resale-Shop / Closed Sunday

Clothes shopping feels a lot better when it's altruistic. Rather than hate myself for denting my bank account every time I splurge, I swing by Encore for a guilt-free shopping spree. The space isn't much to look at; in fact, it's cluttered and could be mistaken for grandma's crazy closet. But the wares are certainly noteworthy, offering a constantly rotating accumulation of clothes. You'll never know what you'll find, be it a Cruella de Vil-esque fur coat or quirky '70s-style pantsuits. What makes this store so worthwhile, though, is its commitment to community. It's a not-for-profit business that receives donated clothes for men, women and children, and uses earnings to support community renewal efforts. Gotta love a store that gives back.

FREDERICK C. ROBIE HOUSE

Architectural history at its finest

5757 South Woodlawn Avenue (at East 58th) / +1 312 994 4000
flwright.org/visit/robiehouse / Closed Tuesday and Wednesday

Touring the Frederick C. Robie House, which is now a museum, feels like exploring a real world *Little House on the Prairie*. It's a distinguished home from architect Frank Lloyd Wright's stellar resume, and is one of the most preeminent examples of Prairie School architecture. This is marked, as you'll see, by the foundation of horizontal lines and the overhanging rooftop eaves. The result looks like something out of a fairy tale, featuring multiple striations of brick exterior, which give way to a rectangular core filled with living spaces, a kitchen and dining room, a billiards room, a butler's pantry, a children's playroom, a servant's wing and more. It's a sight to behold from the outside, but you must take a tour in order to really gauge the full depth of this paragon of Midwestern architecture.

HYDE PARK RECORDS

Soulful vinyl

1377 East 53rd Street (at South Dorchester) / +1 773 288 6588
hydeparkrecords.com / Open daily

Living in an era accustomed to surprise Beyoncé albums and U2 songs automatically downloaded onto our phones whether we want them or not, it's refreshing to see a throwback shop endure. Featuring records stacked floor-to-ceiling in a variety of genres, Hyde Park Records is a musical heaven for vinyl junkies. True to the neighborhood's roots, the crux of the inventory is reserved for jazz, blues and gospel, with albums new and old for the taking. The shop occasionally features an in-store DJ, so you can get a sampling of the wares. Sort of like getting free samples at the food court. Which makes sense, since this stuff is basically food for your soul.

OSAKA GARDEN

Japanese-inspired oasis in Jackson Park

6401 South Stony Island Avenue (inside Jackson Park)
+1 312 742 7529 / gardenofthephoenix.org / **Open daily**

Japan may be a long way away, but you'd never know it once you
step foot into Osaka Garden. Originally designed as part of the
1893 World's Columbian Exposition and named for Chicago's sister
city in Japan, Osaka Garden stands as an apt metaphor for the growing
and fruitful relationship between the US and Japan. It's also known as
The Garden of the Phoenix, which sounds like a Quentin Tarantino movie,
and actually resembles the snowy Japanese garden featured at the end of
Kill Bill... minus the bloodshed, of course. With its idyllic landscape designed
by the legendary Frederick Law Olmsted, the garden is an apt place to Zen
out on the South Side with tranquil lagoons, Japanese plants, islands and
even cherry trees. It's a majestic and calming escape from city life.

THE ORIENTAL INSTITUTE
MUSEUM OF THE
UNIVERSITY OF CHICAGO

The Ancient Middle East, explored

1155 East 58th Street (at South University) / **+1 773 702 9520**
oi.uchicago.edu/museum-exhibits / **Closed Monday**

My fantasy fallback career has always been teaching history. Specifically, Egyptian history. Thanks to *The Mummy* films and required social studies units in junior high, I'm obsessed with the Ancient Near and Middle East, which makes this my nerdy Disney World. Archaeologists who have scoured Egypt, Syria, Israel and Nubia for decades have unearthed artifacts that are housed in this fascinating museum. Art, history and archaeology are well documented and displayed, depicting the world's most ancient civilizations via pottery, sarcophagi, stone sculptures, clay tablets and even remnants of the Dead Sea Scrolls. Be still my heart.

THE PROMONTORY

Hearth-driven American fare

5311 South Lake Park Avenue West (at East 53rd) / **+1 312 801 2100**
promontorychicago.com / Open daily

Eggplant purée smeared on toasty pita. Impossibly tender roast chicken splashed with barbecue aioli. S'more soufflé layered with smoked chocolate, Graham cracker ice cream and brûléed marshmallow. Altogether, it feels like somebody captured my favorite foods and set them over a smoker. The end result is a menu of American cuisine that gives new meaning to comfort food. Everything about The Promontory, a massive multi-level restaurant/bar/music venue, radiates warmth. The hearth oven in the open kitchen lends the sensation of a log cabin furnace; the fire pits on the patio are a reminder of summer camp; the dangling lights draped over the bar recall the glow of a backyard cookout. Everything falls into place so deliciously, so comfortably.

VALOIS

Comforting cuisine fit for a president

1518 East 53rd Street (at South Harper Court) / **+1 773 667 0647**
valoisrestaurant.com / Open daily

Growing up in New Hampshire, my family frequented a diner in downtown Manchester where presidential candidates always stopped to schmooze with locals and normalize over eggs and bacon. It's the type of legendary place where political photos line the walls, and career waiters rattle off menu items as if breakfast is their first language. In Chicago, Valois fills that homesick void. This 90-something-year-old canteen is a favorite for government officials; namely, President Obama when he's in town. Need proof? Check out the photos all over the walls and on the coffee mugs. It's not surprising really, given the cornerstone eatery peddles scrambled eggs, roast beef, Swiss steak, prime rib, pancakes, spaghetti and everything else you'd expect from a cafeteria befitting a homesick head of state.

wintry mix

Where to go when the weather is frightful

CHRISTKINDLMARKET

Winter in Chicago is a beast. After the merriment of autumn wears off, you become acutely aware of just how frostbitten your fingers are becoming, not to mention the daunting ordeal that is living through bitterly cold January, February and March. But since we can't change the weather, we make the most we can of the winter months here.

The glühwein, a hot, spiced red wine, sold at downtown Chicago's annual **Christkindlmarket** will warm both your hands and your soul. Served in commemorative mugs and mini boots, the wine pairs well with the German bounty of hulking schnitzel sandwiches, doughy pretzels and spiced nuts. It's also the perfect place to amass cool wares for the holidays, especially if your friends are interested in intricate grandfather clocks that look like they've been whittled in Geppetto's workshop.

The **One of a Kind Show** is a holiday market so huge it would make Santa's workshop look like a 7-Eleven. One entire floor of Merchandise Mart, a building so enormous it has its own zip code, is devoted to the show, which features a glorious line-up of food vendors, designers, artists and jewelers selling one-of-a-kind goods, all great for gift-giving or selfish hoarding.

Adding a whole new element of excitement to the requisite wintry activity that is ice skating, the "ice ribbon" at **Maggie Daley Park** is one of the coolest (pun intended) outdoor destinations in the colder months. The road-sized rink meanders around the park, offering expansive views of the skyline, Lake Michigan and, of course, adorable wobbly skaters who look like baby deer learning to walk. BYO skates, or rent some for a fee.

If your ideal winter sport is a little warmer than skating, **WhirlyBall** is for you. Combining elements of basketball, lacrosse and bumper cars into one giddy hodgepodge, this is a sport like no other. If the idea of extreme bumper cars is a little too intimidating, the WhirlyBall space also features laser tag, bowling and shuffleboard.

Need a complete escape from the cold, but can't afford a tropical vacation? Head to **Garfield Park Conservatory**. The enormous west side retreat feels like a jungle in the city, lined with passageways that traipse through different climates and landscapes: one room transports to a cacti-filled desert, while another is an Amazonian forest. The glass-ensconced conservatory, awash with sun and greenery, does a body good, especially when the forecast is arctic.

GARFIELD PARK CONSERVATO

CHRISTKINDLMARKET
50 West Washington Street
(between North Dearborn and North Clark)
+1 312 494 2175 christkindlmarket.com
open daily Thanksgiving to Christmas Eve

GARFIELD PARK CONSERVATORY
300 North Central Park Avenue (between West
Lake and West Ferdinand), +1 312 746 5100
garfieldconservatory.org, open daily

MAGGIE DALEY PARK ICE SKATING RIBBON
337 East Randolph Street
(between South Columbus and South Lake Shore)
+1 312 552 3000 maggiedaleypark.com
open daily late-November through March

ONE OF A KIND SHOW
222 West Merchandise Mart Plaza
(between North Wells and North Orleans)
+1 312 527 4141, oneofakindshowchicago.com
open daily December 3-6

WHIRLYBALL
1825 West Webster Avenue (between North Elston
and North Damen), +1 773 486 7777
whirlyball.com open daily